MARTIN LUTHER: A LIFE

MARTIN LUTHER

A LIFE

JAMES A. NESTINGEN

MINNEAPOLIS

With thanks to Gerhard O. Forde,
teacher, colleague, and friend.

MARTIN LUTHER
A Life

Large-quantity purchases or custom editions of this book are available at a discount from the publisher. For more information, contact the sales department at Augsburg Fortress, Publishers, 1-800-328-4648, or write to: Sales Director, Augsburg Fortress, Publishers, P.O. Box 1209, Minneapolis, MN 55440-1209.

ISBN 0-8066-4573-3

Cover and book design by Michelle L. N. Cook
Cover photography by Rolf von der Heydt
Luther photos © 2003 NFP teleart in cooperation with Thrivent Financial for Lutherans
Director: Eric Till / DOP: Robert Fraisse
Producers: Brigitte Rochow, Christian Stehr, and Alexander Thies

The paper used in this publication meets the minimum requirements of American National Standard for Information Sciences—Permanence of Paper for Printed Library Materials, ANSI Z329.48-1984.

Manufactured in the U.S.A.   ♻ ™

07   06   05   04   03   1   2   3   4   5   6   7   8   9   10

CONTENTS

1. From Mansfeld to Monastery: Early Life   7
Prostrate before God ℝ *Many Reputations* ℝ *Early Years*
ℝ *Education and Family Business* ℝ *A Great Dread* ℝ
Monkery ℝ *Dr. Luther* ℝ *Wittenberg*

2. Hunting and Hunted: Luther's Breakthrough   19
Psalms, Epistles, and More Struggles ℝ
The God Who Raises the Dead ℝ *Renewal and Reform*

3. Igniting a Revolution: The Ninety-five Theses   26
"When a Coin in the Coffer Rings . . ." ℝ *Fire Control* ℝ
Theological Rabies ℝ *Luther and Melanchthon at Wittenberg*

4. Breaking Open the Word—and the Church   35
Luther the Theologian ℝ *The Hammer Falls* ℝ
The Diet of Worms ℝ *The Aftermath*

5. The Center Does Not Hold   48
In the Region of the Birds ℝ *The Radicals* ℝ
The Humanists ℝ *The Peasants' War*

6. Luther at Home: Refuge from Chaos   59
Lord Katie

7. Renewal and Reform: 1527–1532   68

More Trouble Within   *Liturgical Renewal and Reform*   *The Catechisms*   *The Makings of an Interlude*

8. Augsburg and Beyond   79

Ecumenical Politics: The Emperor's Efforts   *The Augsburg Confession*   *Augsburg's Aftermath*   *Going Home*   *The Justifying Word*

9. Conflicts and Reconciliations   91

Refining and Redefining the Reform   *Reconciliations on the Upper Rhine*   *Toward a Council: Troubles on the Catholic Side*   *Politics: The Beginning of the End*

10. The End and the Beginning   101

Sick and Tired of Being Sick and Tired   *Some Vicious Attacks*   *Luther and the Jews*   *Calamity in the League*   *Luther's Death*   *The End of the Reformation*

CHAPTER 1

FROM MANSFELD TO MONASTERY: EARLY LIFE

Who was Martin Luther? Pared down to the basics, the answer is surprisingly typical. Born in 1483, he was the son of an upwardly mobile family involved in copper mining. Slated for a career in the law, he disappointed his father by going his own way and becoming a Roman Catholic monk and pastor. Sponsored by the leader of his religious order, the Augustinians, he became Dr. Luther, professor of Bible studies at a small university in the town of Wittenberg; he remained in that position until he died in 1546.

If that were the entire picture of Martin Luther, however, he would reside, like most citizens of the sixteenth century, deep in the shadows cast by contemporary luminaries like Leonardo da Vinci and Michelangelo.

But there is much more to the identity of Martin Luther, enough to make him forever controversial. Through a remarkable chain of events that he could not have anticipated, Luther was lifted from obscurity to the center of the European stage. The battle over who he really was began in his own lifetime, and it has continued ever since.

PROSTRATE BEFORE GOD

As Luther told his own story, it began not with himself but with God, at the point God called him to the religious life.

The call to the religious life played out in a doubly dramatic way. The first drama erupted between father and son when his ordination ceremonies ended: the son driven, haunted, expecting approval; the father tight-faced, proud, but still disappointed. Martin's father, Hans Ludder, had arrived for his son's ordination with a retinue of horsemen and had brought a good sum of money for the community of monks to which his son now belonged. He held his tongue during the service, but as he prepared to leave, he blurted a statement that revealed his reservations about Martin's "call" to the religious life. "I hope it was God" that had called his son, the old man said, "and not the devil." Then he turned and rode away with his men.

But those who had watched closely had also seen another drama, this one hidden in the heart of the twenty-three-year-old monk. In accordance with the traditional ritual, he had lain face down on the floor of the great cathedral in the presence of church officials. As he rose to his knees, hands were laid on his head, words were spoken, and then he stood and went behind the altar where, turning to face the congregation, he began the words of the Mass. He had known them from childhood; he had studied them carefully as he prepared for the priesthood. He knew them all, the priest's statements and the congregation's responses, as well as he knew his own name. But for all the familiarity of the ritual, the words left him in terror. He stumbled, panicky, sure that a sinner like him had no place mouthing such a sacred text. A priest standing with him prompted him, the familiar took over, and he continued, finishing the Holy Communion. But the question of his worthiness wouldn't let go.

MANY REPUTATIONS

Luther has been characterized in many ways—he is the object of extreme admiration as well as scathingly critical and even rude remarks. Some of Luther's followers said he was a brilliant interpreter who had rediscovered the center of the Bible's message. Others said he was a German hero arising to free his people from the oppressions of the Italians and the rest of the Mediterranean world. Some considered him a prophet, like Elijah or John the Baptist, called by God at the end of his days to reform the church. Pope Leo X, the leader of the Roman Catholic Church, had a much different opinion. He called Luther a wild boar ravaging his vineyard. Other Catholics used even more graphic language, denouncing him as the son of a whore and a foul-mouthed drunkard who broke the unity of the church so he could bed down a nun.

Five centuries of study ought to be enough to settle the question of Luther's identity. He left plenty of evidence about himself. He wrote more than 120 volumes, the equivalent of four or five encyclopedias. It would require a huge library to contain all of the studies of Luther's life and thought that have been written since his death. He is one of the most closely examined people in European history. Still, the debate rages.

Was Luther the last medieval man, bent on enclosing all of life into a cast iron, authoritarian system? Was he a virulent anti-Semite who set the foundation for the Holocaust? Or was he the Wittenberg nightingale who sang the first song of a new European morning, an early voice of freedom in the modern world?

Was he an ecumenical theologian, capable of bringing new life to the church? Or was he a haunted manic-depressive who misunderstood the Catholic tradition and led his followers down a dead-end street?

Was he a brilliant poet, hymn writer, and musician who almost single-handedly founded the literary tradition of the German language? Or was he a self-centered loudmouth?

Was he a tender-hearted pastor, or was he a demagogue?

If we could ask Martin Luther to answer for himself, he would probably be characteristically blunt. He once called himself "a bag of maggots, food for the worms." The last words he wrote were: "truly we are beggars." Luther knew himself to be a sinner and generally didn't mince his confessions, even though when challenged about his wrongs he rarely surrendered an inch. As he saw it, his individual image didn't matter—his identity was caught up in and bestowed by Jesus of Nazareth, crucified and risen from the dead.

Will the real Martin Luther please stand up? Given the admixture of reality and legend in his story, the adulation and condemnation in response to his life and writings, the cussedness and tenderness in the man himself, Luther continues to capture people's imaginations. Friend or foe, the fascination makes it worthwhile to take a look at the story. As a public relations agent in New Orleans once remarked, "We advise our clients to tell the truth—it's easier to remember."

EARLY YEARS

Hans Ludder came from a hard-working peasant family near the town of Mohara. They made their living the way farmers still do in most of the world—without the assistance of machinery, by hand and by sweat. Visiting the area today, you can still see people who have the look of Luther and his family—stocky, dark complexioned, strong shouldered, with eyes that are intense, black, and piercing.

But like farm kids around the world, Hans envisioned a different future. Cutting hay by hand, raking it, stooking it, he knew there would be those who would stay at home, taking over the old family responsibilities. He knew, too, that there would be some who would leave, seeking new places and dreams. Hans was one who left. And as he moved, he found an opportunity to improve his chances by marrying above him, into a more prosperous family.

The family name of the woman Hans married is not known with certainty. Most likely, Margarethe Ludder was a daughter or a granddaughter of a prosperous and gifted family named Lindemann. It is also likely that she had run into difficulty finding a husband from her own class. That would have been disappointing for her. But for Hans, his eyes on both her and the future, it was all opportunity.

EDUCATION AND FAMILY BUSINESS

As they set up housekeeping, Hans and Margarethe were eager to give their children all of the advantages they could—and like good German parents in the Middle Ages, they weren't afraid to use discipline to bring out the best in them. Years later, Luther still remembered his mother's stick and his father's sternness, but he also knew the love that went with both. Parents have to use "the apple with the rod," he said—some tenderness to go with the punishments.

Born in the town of Eisleben in 1483, Luther was marked from the beginning for an education. He started school at the age of seven in the town of Mansfeld. There he began to learn a new language. At home, he spoke Middle High German, the dialect of Saxony. At school, he studied Latin, and remembered being punished for not knowing lessons he hadn't been taught yet. He also remembered "the wolf," an older boy assigned to catch others speaking German, and "the jackass"—the poorest student who, at the end of each week, had a board hung around his neck. But Luther learned his cases and declensions and eventually became as at home in Latin as in his mother tongue. In fact, though he didn't care for it when he heard it in others, he could mix up German and Latin with the best of them, shifting from language to language without realizing it, just like generations of North American immigrants who have learned their English in school.

From Mansfeld, Luther went on to schools in two other communities. He spent a year in Magdeburg, one of the great cities of the area, which had 30,000 inhabitants. Then he moved to Eisenach, a much smaller but still important town, where he studied for four years. In Eisenach, Luther literally sang for his supper. Following an old custom, schoolboys roamed the streets, begging for bread by singing. Luther remembered living with Frau Cotta, a woman who looked after him. He also told of a man who yelled down the stairs to the boys singing below and then handed them all a real treat, some sausage. While Luther was going to school, there was another family in Eisenach that would, years later, produce a famous Lutheran. They were church musicians named Bach, and their most illustrious descendant was Johann Sebastian.

When Luther finished his early schooling, he enrolled in the University of Erfurt. The town couldn't match Magdeburg, even if it had more to offer than Eisenach. But the university—which had connections with the University of Prague—was reputedly one of the best. There Luther's academic gifts began to show through. Among his other teachers, he worked with Jodocus Trutfetter, said to be one of the two best logicians in Europe. Trutfetter taught Luther to think clearly, training him in the philosophy called nominalism. (The nominalist position denies the existence of abstract, universal concepts. For example the concept "humanity" has no existence apart from the existence of real human beings.) At Erfurt, Luther also got grounded in another trend of the time, renaissance humanism, which was leading the way in the recovery of purer versions of the ancient languages of Latin, Greek, and Hebrew. But for all of this, Luther's head didn't float away. As part of the curriculum, he began to study the biblical Psalms—working through fifteen a day, he completed the book every ten days and then started all over again. He kept up this practice throughout his life and knew all 150 psalms by heart.

Hans and Margarethe Ludder must have taken a lot of pride in their oldest son. He kept getting better and better academically, finishing a bachelor's degree and then taking a master's, where he really excelled. Hans had another reason to invest his hope in his oldest child. A good vein of copper ore ran through the rocky, rolling lands of what is now east central Germany. Mining it and smelting it into a usable metal offered a man who had learned hard work on the farm a chance for some independence, both financial and personal. But it was risky business, too. The ore had to be located and mining rights secured. Smelting required furnaces, with coal or wood to fire them, and all these resources needed to be found at decent prices. Hans was able to buy his own furnace. But he had learned enough about the conflicts that go with mining rights to know the value of a good lawyer. Having one in the family would go a long way toward the independence he sought.

Following the family plans, Luther started law school in the summer term of 1505. Hans purchased all of the texts for him, and Martin buckled down with his usual level of dedication. But in the meantime, something had happened to young Martin. It would change the direction of his life.

A GREAT DREAD

During the centuries since, the question of exactly what drove Luther to the monastery—and caused the anxieties he betrayed at the altar when he was ordained—has been asked again and again. As he recalled later in his life, a violent thunderstorm brought him to his knees. But the reminiscence of the elderly, helpful and entertaining as they may be, don't always tell the whole story. There must have been more.

Leo Tolstoy, a great Russian writer who lived centuries after Luther, wrote a short story titled "The Death of Ivan Ilyich." In it, he spelled out the common way of thinking about death. The fact that people are mortal, and that therefore a person must die, always seems true in relation to others, he said, but not to the person doing the thinking. No matter how inevitable it might be, the power of death generally seems distant until it strikes close to home.

When that happens, even a young, disciplined, and earnest university student would have to face some hard facts. Maybe an accident, coming from nowhere, snuffs out a life; perhaps a parent dies or has a close call. But all of a sudden, the illusions that shelter us from the reality of death get broken and a person stands exposed, face to face with a destiny that is out of his or her control. At such a point, people start asking questions: What am I doing here? What is my purpose? What am I good for? Where am I going to turn?

Medieval life itself was threatening. A century and a half before Luther's time, the bubonic plague, also called the Black Death, had swept across Europe, killing a third of the population. Though it wasn't as bad in the late fifteenth and early sixteenth centuries, plague still menaced the continent here and there unpredictably. Three of Luther's college friends died of the plague. Writings from Luther's day, when compared with those from more recent times, are more preoccupied with death, impending judgment, and the end of the world. This should come as no surprise, given the historical context. It should also be understandable that small comforts that might satisfy us today would have a hollow ring in Luther's time.

Maybe with Luther, given such a context, it was the Psalms that started the trouble. There are many different types of psalms scattered through the collection assembled in the Bible. Some are hymns of praise, others are poems or songs of thanksgiving or celebration. But there are many now called "psalms of lament," like 77 or 130, that take a person right to the edge of life to peer over the edge, into the bleakness. A steady diet of laments would be enough, all by itself, to challenge one's illusions and make a person wonder about last things and life beyond material existence.

Whatever the state of Luther's mind, certain incidents aggravated his anxieties. One of his schoolmates, a good friend, died suddenly. And then there was an episode with a dagger, the belt knife German university students customarily wore. Luther and a friend were out hunting; Luther fell and drove the dagger into his thigh. The friend ran for help, leaving Luther against a tree with his legs in the air and his hand holding a pressure point in his groin, attempting to staunch the bleeding. Though he recovered fully, death had come close enough that he felt its reality.

Luther's questions compounded themselves, peeling away the illusion of safety. The fear already at large in the later medieval atmosphere turned to dread; the biblical word of lament became a conviction of God's absence from him; the looming force of death appeared to be making him its bull's-eye. The question of his own unworthiness, which betrayed itself at his ordination, became an issue of God's election: What is God doing with me? Am I one of the rejects? Has God withdrawn from me completely, leaving me to myself? Fear and dread, anxiety and consternation tumbled over one another in him, gripping, haunting, driving. Later, Luther used a German word, *Anfechtung*, "a grasping dread," to describe what he felt, and continued to happen to him, throughout his life.

Like the North American prairies, east central Germany can pour down some vicious weather, with enough thunder and lightning to make it seem like the whole world is inescapably ablaze. Luther was on foot one day, near the town of Stotternheim, when he got caught in a torrent. The storm outside matched the conflict raging within himself. Overwhelmed, caught up in his terrors once more, he cried out for protection to the patron saint of miners, "St. Anne, help me, I will become a monk."

Perhaps, in the face of his struggles already underway, Luther had given some prior thought to going to a monastery. Even after the words were wrung out of him, he had some questions about his vow; his friends had even more. His father's doubts were behind the question that spilled out at Luther's ordination—in his mind, as later in Luther's own, the devil could hide in the religious as well as anywhere else. But questions notwithstanding, his terrors receding but capable of breaking out again, Luther left law school behind late in the summer of 1505 and knocked on the door of the Augustinian priory in Erfurt, seeking admission to the order. Legend has it that there had been quite a party the night before, Luther in the lead, singing his high tenor and playing his lute, with lots of beer and some young women, ready for one last adventure. Exaggerations have a life of their own.

MONKERY

Monasticism had a greater presence in Luther's world than it does today. Two types of monasteries and convents seemed to be everywhere in Europe. In the Benedictine-type monasticism, monks and nuns withdrew into their own, usually rural communities, to apply their disciplines of work and prayer. Mendicant orders were a more recent development. These formed smaller groups and lived in the cities, where they supported their work of preaching and service by doing manual labor and begging. Members of monastic and mendicant orders lived according to a "rule" that governed the life and prayer of the community.

Luther was determined to succeed with the Augustinians, a mendicant order that had a monastery in the city of Erfurt. He presented himself there on July 17, 1505. It didn't take long for him to get accepted and established in the community. Devout, earnest, relentlessly self-disciplined, unsparingly self-critical, intelligent, he quickly adapted to monastic life. Taking his share of manual labor, begging in the city with the other monks, he also spent significant time studying. He began what would become voluminous work in Scripture and the theology of the church. As part of his first year as a monk, he was assigned a question intended to help him deepen his acquaintance with the means of grace, the medieval Catholic sacramental system that covered life from birth to death, from baptism to last rites. The question was, How does one find a gracious God? Already troubled by the issue, he worked at it with so much intensity that in later life, he remembered it as his very own question, recalling his dissatisfaction with himself and all of his efforts.

But his troubles didn't affect his performance as a member of the order. Luther was ordained in 1507. Luther caught the attention of the supervisor of the German Augustinians, Johann von Staupitz, who made arrangements for his further education and became his mentor. He became the most important influence in the young monk's life, and Luther prospered under it. He did so well in his studies that he moved right to the head of the class as he prepared for ordination and, later, took the equivalent of another master's degree. Young Martin showed a particular aptitude for the study of the Christian Scriptures. His training in nominalism and humanism had taught him to be suspicious of speculation about God. The Bible, he had learned, provides a much more reliable basis for knowing God and God's intentions. He was so industrious about it, already showing signs of biblical insight, that Staupitz started making some plans for Luther's future—a far different future than Luther himself could have anticipated.

In the meantime, Luther had an adventure away from his books. For some time, the Augustinian community had been struggling with an internal conflict. Some, the "Observants," pressed for stricter standards. Others favored a more lenient, generous application of the rule. Luther sided with the Observants. When Staupitz insisted on a more gentle approach, the Observants appealed his decision to the Augustinian leadership in Rome. In 1510, Luther and one of his Erfurt colleagues were sent to Rome to represent the Observants.

The trip turned into an adventure, even if it was disillusioning. The two brothers walked all the way, the customary means of transportation, going southwest through Germany, across the Alps and Northern Italy to Rome, the eternal city itself—the longest trip Luther ever took. The appeal about the Augustinian rule failed, but Luther took with him some vivid impressions of the church's central city. It was the Rome of some of the most famous men of the Middle Ages—Leonardo da Vinci, recently deceased, and Michelangelo, even then at work on the Sistine Chapel at the Vatican, exacting huge fees while grumbling about being underpaid.

Typically, at least at that time, Luther was more concerned with matters of salvation than with earthly splendors. He remembered speaking the words of the Mass in a slow, deliberate way, while Italian priests whispered, *"Pronto, pronto,"* to speed him up. He also climbed the *Scala Santa* or sacred stairway on his knees, saying the Lord's Prayer on every step, regretting that his mother was still living because such a ritual was said to earn heavenly bliss for anyone the penitent desired. It was his only taste of the world outside of Germany.

DR. LUTHER

Even after Luther returned to Erfurt in January 1511, the controversy in the Augustinian order continued to boil. At this point, however, he had come to support Staupitz's efforts to hold the two sides together.

Perhaps for that reason, later in the year his brothers in Erfurt packed him off to Wittenberg, where Staupitz lived.

Having recognized Luther's gifts as a student of the Bible, Staupitz moved quickly to implement the plan that had begun to take shape year earlier. Initially, Luther didn't much care for the prospect Staupitz unfolded. In fact, he very nearly broke his vow of obedience. But Staupitz was not about to take no for an answer. Pushing his stubborn monk, making arrangements with the faculty in Wittenberg, convincing the head of the government to pay the fees, batting away objections from the brothers in Erfurt, Staupitz made all the arrangements to have Luther promoted to doctor of Scripture.

Luther's hesitations about his worthiness cooled whatever joy he might have had in an academic promotion. As a doctor of Bible, he would be qualified simply to take over the position Staupitz had had on the faculty. But he took part in public debates that demonstrated his qualifications for the degree and won his way instead. Feasting followed along with a formal ceremony in which Luther swore an oath to teach doctrine faithfully.

Later on, Luther looked back on this as one of the most significant moments of his life. Ordination had made him a pastor, setting him apart to preach the word and administer the sacraments. Becoming a doctor of the church, Luther assumed another public office, swearing to uphold the church's witness as well as its theology, its thinking about Scripture, and its tradition. As much as he could downplay the significance of these offices for himself personally, he took great comfort and confidence that God had called him to the offices and the work.

Luther began teaching in 1513. His first lectures were on the Psalms, the biblical poems and hymns he already knew so well. Then he gave lectures on Paul's letters to the Romans and the Galatians. The Romans lectures, beginning in 1515, are some of the most important Luther ever presented.

If professors had to do nothing but teach, they could study to their hearts' content. Luther worked his texts relentlessly, but plenty of other claims also contended for his time. Proud of one of their best and brightest but angry that they had let him get away, the Erfurt chapter kept after him to return. Staupitz gave him some administrative responsibilities—for a while, Luther supervised the monastery in Wittenberg and several others in the area. He was also assigned to preach regularly at the monastery chapel, the town church, and the castle church in the city. With this, Luther also had his turns in the confessional. Every citizen was required to make a full confession of their sins at least once a year, enough to keep all the clergy busy. Luther's personal struggles did not go away, but they did not interfere with his work. With a full monastic routine of prayer and Bible study and the equivalent of two or three full-time jobs, Luther was occupied to the maximum.

WITTENBERG

Walking home from Rome and then moving on to Wittenberg must have been a study in contrasts for Luther. Rome had its connection with the Apostles Peter and Paul; it was the preeminent symbol of ancient civilization and the residence of Christ's vicar on earth, the pope. Wittenberg, or "white mountain," was a little river town in the middle of nowhere, in a part of Germany where the population is more Slavic. With about 2,000 residents, it was considered a dump, with poorly built houses and filthy streets. In fact, one of Luther's later opponents is reported to have said, "No reformation is going to come out of a hole like that."

But appearances don't always tell the whole story; dumpy little Wittenberg was a city on the move. Saxony, the state in which it was located, had been divided into two parts, Electoral Saxony and Ducal Saxony. Frederick the Wise, the leader of Electoral Saxony, was building up Wittenberg as his capital.

Frederick had some real advantages in his project. For one thing, his position gave him a large voice in the political affairs of the Holy Roman Empire, the pretentious name given to the league of cities, duchies, bishoprics, and small states that made up Germany at the time. For another, Wittenberg was far enough away from the bishops to give Frederick some independence with the power structure of the church. Gifted, ambitious, nicknamed "the Wise" because of his even-handedness, Frederick was unknowingly laying the basis for another form of political life, an independent nation-state.

Luther had no more idea than Frederick the Wise of what he was stepping into when he moved to Wittenberg. He, too, had some big advantages in Wittenberg. Back in Stauptiz's good graces, the new professor could count on his superior's direct support as he went about his work. And he had a friend from university days in Erfurt who turned out to be one of Frederick's closest advisors. Georg Spalatin became Frederick's chaplain and was closely involved in the life of the university, which Frederick had founded in 1502 as part of his plan to build up the city. Besides his other duties, Spalatin was effectively the librarian of the university.

Still, Luther had other things on his mind. Keeping up a frantic schedule, gaining a reputation as an effective lecturer and preacher, he was still troubled. In his studies at Erfurt and Wittenberg, he had been taught that God meets with goodness and saving grace people who do everything within themselves that they can do to make a full and honest effort. Luther had striven to do just that, to the point that Staupitz complained, "Every time you fart, you want to make confession of your sins." But Luther still was not convinced of either the completeness of his efforts or the goodness of God.

Luther's close study of Scripture didn't help much, at least until sometime in 1516 or 1517. Sometimes, he caught the drift of something different, of a God in the Bible who gives freely while demanding nothing in return. But it generally went the other way: God's demands became so overpowering that all Luther could see was his unworthiness. Could God have chosen a sinner like him? Hardly. What in the world was a man like him doing, preaching and running a monastery? For all the recognition bestowed by others, he, like a self-conscious adolescent on a date, could see only his own faults.

His story is thus far fairly typical. Yet tucked away in Luther's struggles with his vocation, in his beginnings as a lecturer, in the politics of ugly little Wittenberg, were the ingredients of an explosion.

CHAPTER 2

HUNTING AND HUNTED: LUTHER'S BREAKTHROUGH

Providing for his university required that Frederick the Wise also provide for the Augustinian monks. They had promised to help him build it and had supplied two members of its faculty. So Frederick had been building them a monastery, which was nearing completion. The building included a tower that contained one of the monastery's few heated rooms. Luther, as one of the professors, was entitled to use the room, along with its adjoining sixteenth-century equivalent of indoor plumbing. The close proximity of the two rooms was a source of humor for Luther, as it has been for Lutherans since—his little study and the water closet were side by side. But it has also been the source of some confusion—and there has been more than a little—about what happened to Luther in the course of his studies as he taught between 1513 and 1517.

PSALMS, EPISTLES, AND MORE STRUGGLES

Luther began his work in Wittenberg on familiar territory. As we have seen, he had been working with the Psalms since his days as an undergraduate. Further, monastic life is generally organized around "the hours," set times of prayer throughout the day that feature patterns of Psalms in daily repetitions. One contemporary biographer has commented that it is almost impossible for people of this time to understand how well Luther knew the Psalms—for about a decade, they had formed the warp and woof of his spiritual life, and they would continue to do so as long as he lived. Luther's early series of lectures on the Psalms was followed by another series in 1519 and still others later in his life. When his father died in 1530, Luther turned to Psalm 118 and wrote a beautiful little commentary on it. The early lectures from 1513 and 1514 are an important source for understanding Luther and his reading of Scripture.

Luther was also drawn to the Apostle Paul. Paul has had a checkered career in the life of the church. On the one hand, his letters to his congregations—in Rome, Corinth, Galatia, and elsewhere—were the earliest writings of the New Testament. Time and again, Paul's witness has been a key factor in reshaping and reforming the church. But Paul has also proven troublesome for the church. "Legalists," for example, say that the grace Paul preached is dependent on human striving. "Enthusiasts," on the other hand, believe that grace is a power within that takes people beyond all human limits. But most interpreters of Paul do not fall in either of these clearly defined camps. Instead, they have attributed to Paul a staid, predictable, and generally comfortable view of the world, in which human enterprise is most important. Then, for all of his fire and zeal, Paul becomes bland and routine.

While studying for the priesthood and preparing for his vocation as a professor, Luther had learned about this domesticated Paul. According to this idea of Paul's theology, God takes the initiative, expressing in grace a willingness to forgive sins and to help a person rehabilitate morally. The appropriate response to God's initiative is to "do what it is within you to do," to put forth the best efforts of heart and will to accept the proffered grace and reshape one's personal life accordingly. God doesn't ask anything more than a person is capable of performing; there are certain marks, like humility and moral striving, that give evidence of good effort, and everything works out the way it should.

But Luther's own struggles belied this theory. He was not convinced that his best efforts were sufficient, that he really had done everything that was within him to do. No matter how he disciplined himself, wearing himself out with fasts and relentless self-examinations, he could not be satisfied with his responses.

As he wrestled with himself and spent every waking moment trying to hear the biblical word, another level of trouble beset him. The God of the Psalms and of Paul's witness is not so predictable or domestic. This God sometimes withdraws, stands far off and leaves the faithful in deep suffering. This God is said to choose some peoples of the world, like Israel, while apparently letting others go, leaving them to themselves, their best efforts failing. Maybe Luther couldn't do what was within himself to do because God had not numbered him among the chosen. Perhaps, horrifyingly, God's promise in baptism and the Mass was for other people, but not really for him. There was the dreadful chance that his father had been right, that he had fallen into the hands of the devil and that God had turned against him. The trouble, then, was God, particularly the "righteousness of God," a phrase from the Psalms and from Paul's writings that became Luther's point of focus. In the end, Luther's question was election, God's act of predestining or choosing. Though he himself later remembered it as the monastic question, "How do I find a gracious God?" it was far more complicated: God had broken out of the church's containment policies, gone wild, and judged against Luther, leaving him no place to stand.

There have been many theories and explanations about what really happened to Luther at this point. In fact, unearthing the real source of Luther's struggles has become a minor industry.

Roman Catholics, for instance, suggest that Luther suffered from a common affliction called "scruples," in which an unfounded fear that something that is not a sin, is a sin, compounds the natural introspection of the monk. Catholics also point out, and fairly so, that the nominalism Luther learned did not sufficiently emphasize grace in the way that St. Thomas Aquinas did. Had he known the best form of Catholicism more fully, Luther would have found grace sufficient within it. This theory has recently become popular with Lutherans who, for ecumenical reasons, have wanted to minimize Luther's criticisms of the Catholic tradition.

Another theory takes a psychological approach. In the latter part of his life, Luther often spoke freely about himself while his students took notes. In these comments, often made at dinner tables with ample food and drink, Luther left lots of clues for those who are psychologically minded to analyze in detail. They suggest, for example, that Luther's real problem began with the harsh discipline of his childhood, especially his father's disapproval.

In many and various ways, Luther's afflictions are reduced to personal problems or misunderstandings. In this way he can be dismissed as an aberration or domesticated like the Apostle Paul, the Psalmist, and others who encounter God at the edges of human experience.

THE GOD WHO RAISES THE DEAD

It isn't that easy, though. Death, as we have seen, has a way of intruding upon the illusions that make it seem to be at a safe distance. The routines, rituals, and customary comforts that cloak the ultimate tear open.

Despite every effort, the God of Scripture—who makes alive and takes life, raises up and strikes down, who chooses the faithful and numbers the hairs of every head and follows every sparrow with relentless interest—can and does get loose from our tidy and comfortable categories. The God of Scripture becomes far more a problem than a solution. And then other powers began to show themselves more clearly than they ordinarily do—forces that grip and hold, deep in the heart, in obsessions and compulsions, in the dark side of the soul. At such points, talk of the devil begins to make sense.

In Luther's own language, when this happens the conscience becomes aroused or inflamed. A person's sense of standing in relation to God, neighbor, and life itself gets thrown off balance. Then the ordinary questions from the edge of life—where do I stand? To whom do I belong? Where am I going? Where can I turn?—become almost a form of torture. This doesn't happen to everyone, or with the same intensity. As Luther himself said, it doesn't always last so very long. But people who have stood at the grave of a child know it; so do those who have lost some other life-shaping relationship or have hit bottom with alcohol or some other compulsion. The self becomes both prison and prisoner—there is nowhere to turn.

Desperately hunting, perceiving himself as at the same time as being hunted *for*, Luther pursued his vocation. Frightened, haunted, unable to come to terms with what he read, still he worked. Had his troubles been a matter of misunderstanding the Catholic tradition, he would surely, with his intelligence and discipline, have been likely to overcome it. Had Luther's problem been mental illness, as some psychologists have theorized, he would likely have become incapacitated, which is what commonly happens in such situations. But he never stopped working. Again and again he delved into the very sources that had become so terrifyingly problematic. Finally, something happened—he heard a word from beyond himself, a word that turned it all around.

Luther was studying the phrase that had so troubled him in Paul's Letter to the Romans: "the righteousness of God," or "the justice of God." "I hated this word, 'the justice of God,'" Luther wrote. He had been taught to understand it in terms of the "justice with which God is just and punishes the sinners and the unrighteous."

Luther felt that he was a sinner; he had no confidence that he had pleased God, no matter how conscientiously he lived the life of a monk and doctor of Scripture. He was angry with God; he even admitted to hating "this righteous God." He wrote, "As though it really were not enough that miserable sinners should be eternally damned with original sin and have all kinds of calamities laid upon them by the law of the Ten Commandments, God must go and add sorrow upon sorrow and even through the Gospel itself bring his justice and wrath to bear!"

As he continued to think about the phrase, he wrote, "I noticed the context of the words, namely, 'The justice of God is revealed in it; as it is written, the just shall live by faith.' Then and there, I began to understand the justice of God as that by which the righteous man lives by the gift of God, namely by faith, and this sentence, 'The justice of God is revealed in the Gospel' to be that passive justice with which the merciful God justifies us by faith, as it is written, 'The just shall live by faith.'"

Luther immediately felt "as though reborn." It was a dramatic reversal. Luther had finally heard Paul describe how the God who raised Jesus from the dead goes beyond initiative, beyond offer, beyond passive waiting to actually give what has been commanded: to make the believer righteous, to justify, to complete what has already been begun by creating faith. The God Luther had sought to control with his own "understanding or effort," "reason or strength," had turned on him in sheer, unqualified goodness, promising him to make him God's own.

With this, Luther's conscience came to rest, at least for a time. The relationship that had been distorted was restored. God had turned to him, keeping the promise of baptism and the Lord's Supper; God was making him the person Luther was intended to be so he could go to his neighbors and live as a person of the earth, joyfully. He was justified.

Of course, the great dreads—the affliction that had long pursued him—would return to reassert their claim once more. But Luther now had a sense of the rhythm of life in Christ. It was and is, as Paul said, a broken meter—a dance of dying with Christ in the crucifixions of everyday life to be also raised with him to newness of life—life in faith.

RENEWAL AND REFORM

Luther's breakthrough with the biblical word has often been called his "tower experience." As he later recalled, that is where it happened, most likely in his room while he was studying. Scholars who study Luther's life and work have spilled a lot of ink debating the date of his discovery. It most likely occurred late in 1516. The question remains open, however, because many statements in Luther's earlier work sound like what he came to, and many statements after 1516 seem to be arguing against his own breakthrough. Most likely, it didn't happen all at once—the breakthrough came after some preparation, and it took awhile to sort out all of the implications.

But one thing that did happen for sure was that Luther developed a new perspective on preaching. His struggle was personal but his vocation was public. As a doctor of the church, he had taken an oath faithfully to serve the church in its study of Scripture and in its witness. At the university, he was called to assist in the preparation of pastors. So having heard the promise of the God who raised Jesus from the dead, his immediate goal was to give it away to any and all who would hear it, starting with his students, and beyond them, the parishes they would be serving.

The center of medieval Roman Catholic church life was the Mass, the sacrament of the altar. Now, however, the center had shifted. Luther had heard a word, a living, powerful, life-bestowing word bearing the force of God's new creation. That word is spoken in the words of institution in the celebration of Holy Communion: "Our Lord Jesus Christ, on the night in which he was betrayed, took bread. . . ." But this word is also present in preaching. In fact, as Luther heard it, the word is the very purpose of preaching, not merely to communicate information or to appeal to people's wills, but actually to give the gifts and benefits of Christ Jesus. Having heard that word break through to him, Luther set out, in the training of new pastors, to improve their preaching.

But something else happened as well. Like Peter facing up to his own denials of Christ, Luther, having heard the word of Christ's death and resurrection, began to see the emptiness and self-absorption, the pious pretense and unbelief, of all of his prior striving. Looked at in the light of Christ, he knew himself a sinner.

But he also saw pious fraudulence in the world around him. It didn't take an extended examination. Late medieval life was religiously saturated, piety marked virtually every aspect of life. There were church-sanctioned butter laws and meat regulations, stipulating how much could be eaten and when. An industry of indulgences had been built up around the confessional, giving penitents a way to purchase forgiveness. In all of this, a person could hardly turn around without encountering an emaciated mendicant's outstretched palm. The church spread a pious veneer over many aspects of European life.

Like the humanists he had studied early in his academic career, Luther protested all such pieties and practices. He did it quietly at first, in conversations among friends and with his students. But the further he delved into God's sweeping goodness, the more energized his protests became.

Maybe, in another time, in another place, the story would have ended differently. Perhaps Luther would have launched some symbolic protest and, recognizing the inevitable, gone back to his classrooms and the monastery. Perhaps he would have had a distinguished career as a teacher. He would likely have succeeded Staupitz, his mentor. He would very likely have contributed greatly to the improvement of preaching, which was one of his primary goals. Even his father might have had enough reason to be proud of him. And then he would have found his way into obscurity, with all the rest.

But dumpy little Wittenberg with its university—the equivalent of a small state teacher's college—turned out to be a dynamite closet. The town printer, who toiled in the monastery basement learning to exploit a newly developing mass medium, turned out be a bombardier. And Luther unwittingly struck the match by promoting public discussion of religious exploitation. By the time the smoke cleared, Luther had become—for all intents and purposes, and by accident—a church reformer. It was hardly a calling he sought.

CHAPTER 3

IGNITING A REVOLUTION: THE NINETY-FIVE THESES

On All Hallows' Eve or Halloween—October 31, 1517, Martin Luther reportedly went to the church door in Wittenberg, which functioned as the university bulletin board, and nailed a set of propositions to debate the practice of granting indulgences. His propositions have been called the *Ninety-five Theses:*

> When our Lord Jesus Christ said, "Repent," he willed the entire life of believers to be one of repentance. . . .
>
> Any truly repentant Christian has a right to full remission of penalty and guilt, even without indulgence letters.
>
> Any true Christian, whether living or dead, participates in all the blessings of Christ and the church; and this is granted him by God, even without indulgence letters. . . .
>
> The treasures of indulgences are nets with which one now fishes for the wealth of men.

Luther's historic posting is sometimes thought legendary, but there's no doubt at all about something else he did. He assumed that the new archbishop, Albert of Mainz, responsible for the overall religious life of his territory, would want to know about some of the abuses of this practice. Only a monk, and a pious one at that, would be likely to make such an assumption. Fatefully, Luther sent a copy of his theses to the archbishop, and he gave a copy to the Wittenberg printer.

That was the match that ignited it all. Printed, copied, and reprinted by any number of small print shops, the theses caught the imagination of disgruntled critics of the church all over Germany and beyond. In little more than two weeks, copies were showing up in the Netherlands, France, and even Italy and Spain.

"WHEN A COIN IN THE COFFER RINGS . . ."

On paper, indulgences don't look that objectionable. The basic idea is simple. A sin against God—something like drunkenness or adultery—is at the same time, a sin against the community. For centuries, the church had seen itself as not only announcing God's forgiveness to sinners but also gauging and dispensing the punishments that sinners must endure—in this life or in the afterlife in a state called purgatory—before being with God in heaven. In Luther's day, this happened in the confessional, where the priest assessed the sinner's contrition and then meted out the required satisfaction. An indulgence takes the place of some other form of penance. So, having undertaken a pilgrimage or made some other sacrifice, financial or otherwise, the penitent could obtain indulgences that could then be used to satisfy penalties for oneself or for a deceased soul. It was a system deeply vulnerable to abuse, and Luther's growing conviction about how little we merit our salvation was profoundly offended by the moral calculus of indulgences.

But there is good money in bad religion. When there's cash available and when there's a huckster loose, the subtleties of the system can easily be forgotten. So John Tetzel, a Dominican friar legendary for his ability as an indulgence salesman, set up shop outside of Wittenberg to preach indulgences and raise money for the building of St. Peter's basilica in Rome. He is reported to have said that by purchasing one of his indulgences, even someone who had raped the blessed Virgin herself could be assured of salvation. The slogan was, "When a coin in the coffer rings, a soul from purgatory to heaven springs," and it came complete with lurid portrayals of dead relatives waiting urgently in purgatory for someone to buy their release.

As it turned out, however, Tetzel's selling of indulgences was not the only form of corruption in the church. The Roman Catholic Church was the most powerful institution in medieval Europe, the one multinational corporation. For all the good it did, the church also had had persistent difficulties with a couple of abuses, lay *simony* and *investiture*. They went together. When a position in the church was open, it was effectively put up for bids—that is simony (named for Simon the Magician, who attempted to purchase the miracle-working power of Peter and Paul).

The clergy didn't always have the necessary money to be good bidders. So the auction was opened to the laity, particularly the wealthy, who could bid in the confidence that they would recoup their costs with the income assigned to the office. If the bid were successful, ordination would be arranged later. In fact, many bishops and even some popes were ordained after their election. That is lay *investiture*. Albert of Mainz had become archbishop in just this way, by bidding on the office.

Tetzel's presence was a three-way arrangement, involving the papacy, Albert of Mainz, and his bankers. The papacy's remodeling of St. Peter's was at considerable expense. Michelangelo might not have charged overtime, but he didn't come cheap either. When Albert expressed interest in the archbishopric, papal officials helped him set up financing with a famous banking family from Augsburg, in the south of Germany, named the Fuggers. Tetzel was retained also to help pay off Albert's mortgage, which helps to explain both his quick response to Luther's protest and the fact that he so promptly forwarded it to Rome.

There were complications in Wittenberg as well. Frederick the Wise was a noted relic collector. He had gathered body parts of various saints and other sacred objects, the collective sight of which was said to bestow some 30,000 years worth of indulgences. Frederick wouldn't let Tetzel preach in Wittenberg because he didn't want the competition. So Luther's attack on the indulgence traffic didn't make his elector any happier than it made his archbishop.

Yet Luther did not back down. Throughout his life as a teacher and a pastor, he clung closely to his call. He didn't get into this voluntarily, he said, but acted only as called by God and by the community. But as both his father and Staupitz had learned, Luther stuck by his convictions. As the church and its allied authorities escalated the case against him, each time he matched and raised them, along the way spelling out ever more radically the implications of his biblical interpretation. The resulting conflict made the years between 1517 and 1521 the most dramatic of his life, and the most exciting of the Reformation.

Frederick also knew what Luther's sudden fame could mean to his university. So, with Spalatin urging him on, Frederick protected Luther despite his own apprehensions about Luther's teachings. If he hadn't, Luther's fate would have been the same as any number of other would-be reformers, accidental or intentional. In all likelihood it would have been all over as quickly as it began, in a heretic's death.

FIRE CONTROL

In the years following the explosion out of Wittenberg, Roman Catholic officials made several direct efforts to contain the damage. The archbishop of Mainz smelled danger and quickly reported the situation to Rome. He then dropped out of things after he handed the issue over to the *curia*, who are church officers gathered around the pope. Luther and others called them "the papists"; today they would be called church bureaucrats. It was in their interest to protect the institution to the best of their ability, and so they moved against Luther, if not in any organized way, with increasing force.

The first effort came through Luther's own Augustinian order. A chain of command stretched all the way from Wittenberg to Rome, where the Vicar General of the Augustinian order, Cardinal Volta, resided. He and the rest of the leadership had lots of experience dealing with monks who thought of themselves as prophets. In fact, he or maybe one of his assistants may have remembered Luther's earlier visit to Rome. Volta was alerted to the indulgence trouble, and he in turn contacted Johann Staupitz, with orders to stifle the young monk.

This put Staupitz in an awkward situation. Luther had become something like a son to him. The two of them had spent many hours together, particularly in the depths of Luther's struggles with his faith and his dread. Mentoring him, Staupitz had consoled his brilliant young colleague with thoughts of the crucified Christ. Luther had found this counsel very helpful, especially when thoughts of God's judgment were bearing down on him, and he credited his supervisor and friend for his aid. Staupitz wasn't so sure of all the implications of Luther's bold theses, but he still had strong loyalties—to Luther as well as to his superiors, to whom he owed obedience.

Staupitz tried to satisfy both loyalties by assigning Luther to give the featured lecture at the annual gathering of the German Augustinians, scheduled for Heidelberg in April 1518. That way, Luther would still get his opportunity to elaborate on his points but in a safe context, with his other brothers around to correct and contain him. So Luther and his Wittenberg colleagues walked down to Erfurt, on to Leipzig, and, catching occasional cart rides, traveled all the way, more than two hundred miles, to the great university city. There Luther offered another set of theses, further defining what he had come to in his studies. Called the *Heidelberg Disputation*, these propositions are still some of the most important and powerful summaries of his new way of thinking. Martin Bucer, who later became an important reformer in the city of Strasbourg, always remembered how Luther's black eyes flashed during the discussion. By all accounts, Luther's lecture was enthusiastically received, and Staupitz's containment strategy failed.

The second effort to contain Luther's fire involved Frederick the Wise. With the church lacking strong representation in Wittenberg, with no bishop who would step in and do what Staupitz hadn't been able to accomplish, the elector was the only available alternative. Luther needed Frederick's protection from the church hierarchy. And, of course, Frederick could be counted on to know the practicalities of power at that time, which generally involved generous amounts of cash—what would now be termed bribery. A Saxon nobleman well-acquainted in both Rome and Wittenberg was dispatched from Rome to have a conversation with the elector. In the course of the visit, he told Frederick that the pope was interested in rewarding him for his loyalty and service by giving him a coveted papal decoration, the Golden Rose, which included substantial cash. In the bargain, Frederick could name the person of his choice as his bishop, with the understanding that the new bishop might be Luther. Frederick knew his politics and the importance of finances, but he wouldn't be bought.

The third and most dramatic effort to put out the fire ignited in the indulgence controversy involved one of the most prominent theologians in Rome, Thomas Cardinal Cajetan. A distinguished Italian gentleman, he was also a leading member of the Dominicans, the mendicant order to which the most illustrious theologian, Thomas Aquinas, had belonged. Cajetan was the leading interpreter of Thomas's thought at that time—in fact, likely the best between the thirteenth and twentieth centuries. His commentaries are still studied. For the first time since the conflict began, Luther would get the chance to meet with someone capable of understanding the theological and biblical roots of his provocative theses.

Luther and Cajetan met in October 1518 in the city of Augsburg. Though richly paternal, well aware of his superior standing, Cajetan did give the rough-talking miner's son more than he had previously gotten, a genuine hearing. More than anyone else, maybe even Luther himself, Cajetan understood the implications of Luther's deep and growing reservations about Catholic tradition and practice. Yet he was shocked, both by Luther's apparent impertinence in the face of Cajetan's authority and by the depth of their theological difference. Sensing this, Luther was keenly aware that this meeting was far more dangerous than a simple discussion. Even though Luther had a promise of safe conduct, assuring him of his protection, Cajetan had the authority to arrest him.

Luther well remembered, as did his friends, what had happened to a Czech reformer, Jan Hus, who used a safe conduct to attend a conference set up under the pretext of mutual understanding. He was burned at the stake. So, knowing their inequality of power and recognizing that Cajetan found his positions disturbing, Luther took a horse that had been provided for him and escaped by night.

Though others earlier had clearly sensed the possible damage to indulgence sales, Cajetan was the first and only church official to see the wider dimensions of Luther's protest. Still, he, Tetzel, and another authority closely involved—Sylvester Prierias, the official papal theologian—were all Dominicans. The most plausible explanation of the trouble was to treat it as another in a long line of conflicts between monastic orders—in this case, Dominicans versus Augustinians. The measures taken to contain Luther are familiar enough, even now in large organizations—first argument and suasion, then institutional and political pressure, with the implicit and final threat of force.

THEOLOGICAL RABIES

While dealing with the official or semi-official attempts of the Roman *curia* to contain his cause, Luther was caught up in a series of bitter battles with other theologians. Something about church councils and annual meetings brings out the bad side in people, even (or especially) in the pious. Theologians can be even worse. Generally intelligent and learned, they are commonly convinced that they know what is best for the church and are frustrated by their inability to impose their own way. So they turn on one another fiercely and, just as often, with generous measures of deception.

Even so, sixteenth-century theologians still hold a record for their outspoken, outrageous attacks on one another. Theological attacks were excessive, colorful, frequently humorous, and regularly dirty. Linguistically gifted in a graphic way and possessed of a sense of humor that didn't always recognize appropriate limits, Luther was one of the best of theological polemicists. He, for example, regularly elided the title and the name of one of his perpetual opponents, Johann Eck. Dr. Eck became Dreck—manure, to translate it politely.

Eck was among the first, though hardly the best, of Luther's theological opponents. Among the most long-lasting, he attacked Luther regularly in print and occasionally winning a place with the politicians in efforts to stop him. Eck hung on into the 1540s. In one of their most famous engagements, he and Luther met face-to-face to debate one another in the city of Leipzig in 1519. That part of Germany is not so far from Prague, where the fifteenth-century reformer Jan Hus had marshaled wide support for a moral overhaul of the clergy. He was the one whose safe conduct carried him to the stake. The memory was still fresh enough that Hus had sympathizers, not only in what is now the Czech Republic but in Germany as well. Church and political leaders considered the Hussites a threat. In the debate, which was attended by the faculty of the university and lasted ten days, Eck attempted to paint Luther as a logical successor of Hus. True to form, when pushed, Luther accepted the comparison. He remarked that there were things about Hus's way of thinking that were worthwhile, a remark that didn't endear him to the authorities. Duke George, who ruled the other part of Saxony, was particularly alarmed. The debate at Leipzig publically aired Luther's positions on a whole array of issues but most bitterly on the issue of papal authority.

Another opponent of Luther at this time was Jerome Emser, a clergyman who served Duke George and had his support for taking Luther on. They squared off in a series of essays, particularly on interpretation of the Bible. Taking his cue from the goat in Emser's coat of arms, Luther wrote "To the Goat Emser," escalating the insult in subsequent replies until he was writing "Hyperlearned, Hyperspiritual Goat Emser." Outspoken, even outrageous as they were, Luther's polemics still showed compelling evidence of his careful theological discipline. He was building his case, thinking through the further implications of his position on indulgences and other church abuses, as well as the issues of scriptural interpretation and papal authority.

Though they were unable to bring Luther to submission theologically, his opponents also worked through other means. Eck approached Frederick the Wise directly, seeking to undercut Frederick's support of Luther. Though he didn't succeed, the pressures led to some conflict between Luther and Spalatin that was troubling for Luther. Eck and Emser sought the judgment of other theological faculties. Transcripts of the Leipzig Debate were submitted to the faculty at Erfurt, which eventually ruled in Eck's favor, much to Luther's dismay. Two other theological faculties in Europe, at Cologne in Germany and Louvain in present-day Belgium, also denounced Luther.

LUTHER AND MELANCHTHON AT WITTENBERG

In the meantime, however, Luther was also gathering significant support close at hand, in Wittenberg itself. The most important came from an unlikely source, a young, slight, lisping linguist who arrived at the university in 1518. He had Latinized his given name, Philip Schwarzherd, to make it Melanchthon—both words mean "black dirt." Well trained in ancient languages, Melanchthon at twenty-one had a full academic pedigree. He had been denied a master's degree at Heidelberg on the basis of age—he was then fourteen—and finished his education at one of the greatest German universities, at Tübingen.

Melanchthon and Luther were in many ways opposites. Even in the midst of all of the conflicts, official or unofficial, Luther was still very much a pastor, preaching regularly, carrying out other pastoral responsibilities. He was outgoing, explosive, tender, and sometimes harsh, emotional but also determined in a conflict. Melanchthon was an academic thoroughbred, pastorally concerned but never ordained, a Greek and Latin professor who eventually took a chair in the theological faculty. He ably represented the humanist tradition, with its high regard for the classics, for working in original languages, and for promoting human values of freedom and dignity. He was also close, careful, and more reserved than Luther, even if he could be vindictive and forceful when he deemed it necessary. Despite their differences, Luther and Melanchthon formed a close and intriguing friendship, learning from one another, agreeing at the center even as they eventually came to some substantial differences. In the end, it was Melanchthon who preached Luther's funeral sermon.

When Melanchthon arrived in Wittenberg, his first lecture was on, of all things, curriculum reform. Despite everything else he had on his mind, Luther was immediately taken with the lecture. They set about reshaping the school's offerings based on Melanchthon's humanist model, giving particular emphasis to languages and biblical studies rather than the traditional "scholastic" offerings centered on logical, philosophical, and theological theses. For a time, Luther served as dean of the faculty.

Luther and Melanchthon were joined by other friends. One was Nicolas von Amsdorf, closer to Luther's own age than Melanchthon. He had been trained at the University of Cologne and in his later years became for a while superintendent or bishop in the city of Magdeburg. Another was Johann Agricola, a medical student from Leipzig who moved to Wittenberg during the indulgence controversy. In later years, he became an opponent of Luther—some have said because Melanchthon got the appointment to the theological faculty that Agricola had wanted. In the early years, Luther, Melanchthon, and Agricola were something like the three musketeers; Agricola later divided from them on the place of the law in the church's witness. Still others, arriving early or along the way, were John Bugenhagen from Pomerania, the city pastor whom Luther nicknamed affectionately "Dr. Pommer"; and Justus Jonas, a member of the law faculty who was also a hymn writer. Bugenhagen became Luther's confessor and played a critical part in carrying the Reformation to Denmark.

Through all of this, Luther continued to teach. He followed up his earlier interests, studying especially Paul and the Psalms. His 1518 lectures on Galatians were published, as was a 1518–1519 course in Psalms. The elector Frederick's anticipation of Luther's impact on enrollment at his university turned out to be accurate. At one point in 1519, Luther was lecturing to more than four hundred students.

CHAPTER 4

BREAKING OPEN THE WORD— AND THE CHURCH

E ven in the midst of his many duties as pastor and teacher, and as controversy swirled around him between 1518 and 1521, Martin Luther was coming to a deeper insight about the central convictions that would radically alter the world.

LUTHER THE THEOLOGIAN

Martin Luther never wrote a complete theological system. Unlike John Calvin, the great French reformer of a later generation who began with a set of doctrinal assumptions and elaborated on them in a full treatise, Luther worked strategically. As he had been trained to do, Luther began with distinctions he understood to be required by God's justifying work. He applied these distinctions to the particular situation he was working in, thinking them through as the occasion demanded.

Another term for this way of thinking is *dialectical*. It is a cliché to say that life is like a pendulum, swinging from one extreme to another, the goal being to find the happy middle. Luther, who lived before such confidence developed, was not at all sure that the middle could be found or should be valued. Instead, he looked for the two sides, the extremes, and set them over and against one another. Truth comes out of the dialectic, that is, from the way in which two extremes butt up against one another to limit or to establish each other. So Luther's way of thinking features distinctions that work in opposing pairs—law and Gospel, for example, or two kinds of righteousness, the two kingdoms, or the Christian's life as saint and sinner.

This way of thinking can make it difficult for Luther's readers. He is paradoxical, so that it often seems as though he is contradicting himself, saying one thing in one situation, something completely different in another. The trick to understanding Luther is to find the pairing and to catch the way the contradictions work on one another and how they develop out of the first Gospel, God's gracious act in Christ Jesus. In the New Testament, for example, there is a dialectic at work: the cross and the resurrection go together, inextricably paired. There is no resurrection without a cross, no cross without a resurrection.

This way of thinking also challenged Luther, even if he relished the task. He did not arrive from his tower experience with some system or program, just needing slight modification before it could be fit to any circumstance. He had to think and rethink, filling in the implications as he took up each issue and then going through the whole process all over again. This process was necessary because Luther was not dealing with an object that could be measured, nailed down, or tested by repetition. He was thinking about a subject, the living God, the Lord Jesus raised from the dead, and God's Spirit, who comprehends us even as we are trying to figure out what God is doing in our lives now.

The result was that Luther's way of thinking theologically continued to change and develop, particularly between 1517 and 1521, when he was attempting to articulate the meaning and implications of what he had concluded in his study of Scripture. His consistency is something like that of a theme and variations in classical music or jazz. The fun comes in suddenly hearing the melody emerge once more.

While he was fighting his way through the indulgence controversy, early in 1518, Luther was thinking through the meaning of Christ's death and resurrection for the life of the believer. In several writings from this time, but especially in the *Heidelberg Disputation,* he set up a contrast between a theology of glory and a theology of the cross. The issue, after all he had been through, was basic: How do human beings really come to know God?

The ordinary answer, which Luther calls a theology of glory, is to take it for granted that people are the acting subjects and that God is an object, to be found and studied like other objects. Such knowledge is the mind's equivalent of a good work, a personal achievement. In contrast, a theology of the cross begins with Christ's death and resurrection. We come to know God, Luther believed, as God actively takes us more deeply into the contradictions and suffering of everyday life. There we lose our grip on ourselves and everything around us, and all our complacencies are broken. Having put us to death, so to speak, God then raises us to newness of life through faith in him. There is a brokenness, a breach, a discontinuity—the old sinner in each of us, for whom knowledge of God is the equivalent of control of God, gets brought to an end. The new self, released from its striving and "achievements," can then begin to move freely in the grace of God's limitless goodness.

Luther's argument differs from traditional theology. He does not deduce from a set of philosophical premises but elaborates on a personal encounter with the Gospel. He does not pair the theology of glory and the theology of the cross as opposites, each having its essential place. The theology of the cross is clearly the way of knowing, definitive for the Christian faith.

As he worked his way through Paul's Letter to the Galatians in his first set of lectures on that book in 1516–1517 and took up the Psalms once more, a new theme began to emerge. It is reflected in the different spelling of Luther's name. Martin Ludder or Lutter became Martin Luther, a small change based on the Greek word for freedom, *elutherius.* As Gerhard Ebeling, a great Luther scholar, pointed out, Luther's best writing is all devoted to the theme of freedom.

With this change, Luther also turned to a different audience—one that he had addressed in his preaching but which now also became a particular concern in his writing. To this point, he had written mostly in answer to church officials or in his feuds with various theologians. Though he continued to write for other academics, after 1517 he began to address pamphlets directly to the laity.

It was a critically important move. Gutenberg's printing press, developed in the middle of the fifteenth century, was no competition for a modern copier or a computer printer. It was built on a thick pole with large threads for screwing down a pressure plate to make an impression on another plate holding the moveable type and paper—hard work that left printers with overdeveloped torsos and muscular arms. Although primitive, the machinery was becoming more widely available. And there were plenty of men—often academics who hadn't been able to find a place on a faculty—willing to ply the trade.

There were readers, too. By modern, Western standards, literacy rates were pretty low. Before print and in its early days, only the privileged learned to read. But then, as now in many parts of the world, communities and neighborhoods could get the services of a reader, someone who would read aloud.

And there was an audience. Mushrooming population growth, as Europe recovered from the losses of the Black Death, was forcing a new class of people off the farms into the developing cities of Germany. There were roughly sixty cities, some of them small, like Wittenberg; only one, Cologne, being really large. Moving away from farms on which their families had worked for generations, these people were reexamining old traditions, trying to come to terms with a new way of life in the crafts and guilds, where they provided labor. They had plenty of hard experience with the dominance of the church and they were sympathetic to critics like Luther.

Many of these early publications were *Flugschriften* ("flying writings"), or what today we would call pamphlets. Short and quickly set up to print, small and easily carried, these publications could be rapidly disseminated, and they weren't hard to conceal, should authorities become aware of what was being read. There weren't any modern means of transportation, but there was regular foot traffic between the cities. And there weren't any copyright laws, either. Anything in print was fair game, especially if it excited enough popular interest to command a decent price.

Martin Luther quickly became a printer's dream. Hans Luft in Wittenberg had his print shop in the monastery basement—as often as not, he would be setting the beginning of a pamphlet in type while Luther was upstairs writing the end of it. But neither of them could keep up with the demand. At one point in the 1520s, three-quarters of the material in print in Germany had been written by Luther. The farmers provided some of Luther's most important early support; the new city dwellers stayed with him through the whole Reformation and after. When the authorities did come against him with force, Luther's many readers gave pause to civil and church authorities.

A number of Luther's sermons were put out in print, including *Two Kinds of Righteousness,* which is helpful for understanding what was happening in his theology. He wrote essays on the sacraments and on penance. Three pamphlets, each written in 1520, were especially important and influential. They also show how Luther continued to develop theologically, especially around the theme of freedom.

The first of these key essays was *To the German Nobility.* For at least a couple of centuries, particularly since the fourteenth century, when two and even three popes sometimes ruled simultaneously, there had been questions about the way in which the church was governed. Looking back to the church council in the biblical Book of Acts 15 and the ecumenical councils in the early centuries, some theologians argued that that was the way things should work, through meetings of the bishops. Leo X, pope at the time, had been elected to overhaul the papacy so it worked more effectively. In *To the German Nobility,* Luther insisted that the church does not belong to the hierarchy—pope, cardinals, bishops, and priests—but having been created by God's word, belongs to all who hear it. With this, he urged the German political leadership to do exactly what Frederick the Wise was doing by taking a hand in the leadership of the church and recalling it to its purpose.

The Babylonian Captivity of the Church, the second of the three treatises, tackles the details of reform. In Roman Catholicism, there are seven sacraments—baptism, confirmation, confession or penance, the Mass or eucharist, marriage, ordination, and anointing of the sick. In Luther's mind, as in the minds of the other reformers, the key problem was the Mass, which reenacts the Last Supper of Jesus with his disciples. It had been reinterpreted over the centuries as a sacrifice. Just as Jesus offered himself as the bloody sacrifice on Calvary, so in the Mass the priest offered Jesus as an unbloody sacrifice—Jesus being really present in the changed ("transubstantiated") elements of bread and wine. In the eyes of the people, the clergy derived their authority from the Mass—only they, ordained by the church through its bishops—could legitimately consecrate the elements and offer up the sacrifice. And through the Mass, the church claimed an authority beyond any other institution. It became the indispensable source of the grace or merits earned by Christ's death, an infinite treasury of grace that it in turn distributed to the faithful. At the worst, Masses became a spiritual commodity, to be bought and sold.

As Luther examined the sacramental system in light of his biblical study, he became convinced that things were turned around. The Mass is not a sacrifice but a sacrament, not an act of the church carried out through the clergy but the Lord's Supper in which the Spirit of the risen Christ distributes his gifts to sinners. So in *The Babylonian Captivity* he worked his way through the seven sacraments, pointing out that Jesus had in fact instituted only two, Baptism and the Lord's Supper. He was still thinking about penance: at the beginning of the treatise, it is the third sacrament; at the end he isn't so sure. But he remained convinced all his life that confession and absolution are a process in which Christ works through the word to assure people of pardon and release. So just like *To the German Nobility,* the second of the treatises, *The Babylonian Captivity,* worked to renew and reform key institutions of the Christian church.

The third treatise from 1520 is called *On Christian Liberty* or *The Freedom of a Christian*. It was quickly recognized as one of the classic statements of Luther's position. Working in his dialectical way, he sets up two statements that seem mutually contradictory: "The Christian is the perfectly free lord of all, subject to none," and "The Christian is the perfectly dutiful servant of all, subject to all." Both statements are true, and each requires the other. In Christ, the Christian has been set free from the powers of sin, death, and the devil—the forces of desolation that grasp and bind by turning the self in on itself. So, like a lover with the beloved, a believer moves freely, confidently, expectantly, oblivious to demands, rules, and regulations. But at the same time, there is the beloved—and with that one, who is so all-determining, the neighbor in need of service. So the believer turns to the needs and necessities, the obligations and responsibilities of everyday life, giving oneself freely in service.

Luther uses the word *freedom* differently than it is now commonly understood. Particularly in the United States, freedom is political and personal: it is freedom of choice, the right to make your own decisions and follow your own lead. Luther used the word in a deeper way, to speak of the liberty that arises in the deepest relationships of life, in faith, hope, and love. It is freedom *from* paralysis of the will, *from* compulsion, and even *from* choice, when the believer is so gripped and held by the love of Christ and the neighbor that there is literally no alternative. This is like the liberty of a long and happy marriage that holds together even in conflict, or the attention of someone so deep in the groove of some hope that everything else becomes irrelevant. It is what happened to Luther as the word took hold of him and what happens again and again as Christ asserts his tender grip. As the account of the Transfiguration in the Gospel says of the apostles, "They saw nothing but Jesus only."

With this, Luther had filled in the other side of the dialectic. Through his early life, in his early efforts as a monk and a professor, he had fought with the powers at work in himself until finally he heard the word of Christ's promise. That had been the issue through the early years of what became the Reformation, as well—to defend Christ's promise in the face of every attempt to diminish or dismiss it in favor of some other authority. Now Luther was filling out the dimensions Christ's promise takes in the life of faith. Accordingly, in *The Freedom of a Christian*, as in the sermon *Two Kinds of Righteousness*, he takes up what would become a theme of his future work: the vocation of everyday life, the service of the faithful.

THE HAMMER FALLS

In the years between 1517 and 1520, all of the efforts of churchwide authorities, theologians, and faculties to stifle Luther had proven counterproductive. With scarcely a clue concerning the impact of his actions, Luther had set off an explosion in the indulgence controversy that had echoed all the way through Germany and into surrounding countries. Nothing had been able to contain it. Given the realities of late medieval life, the next move was predictable: the authorities would resort to force, as they had with every other reforming movement that resisted absorption and stilling.

As Luther reviewed the events of the past years, he saw them as a preacher would, in the light of eternity. Conflict is what always happened when the word of God got loose in ancient Israel, in Jesus' life, and in the life of the early church. It happened to the prophets and to Jesus himself. They became the issue; they were rejected and, in the end, put to death. As Luther understood it, there could be only one explanation of both his widespread support and the trouble that had gone with it: it was the word, reforming the church.

Clearly, things were stirring. Germany had been for centuries a boondocks, a region useful to the southern Europeans for its resources and manpower but backwards and out of touch. Luther's protests had released long-term, festering resentment among the Germans, and those social, political, and economic forces had now coalesced around him. Farmers and the new populations of former farmers moving into the cities heard Luther gladly, picking up his protest through the pamphlets. The mainstays of medieval life were breaking down, straining at its limits; a new way of understanding and interpreting public and personal life was emerging. Luther had been caught up and carried along in forces bigger than himself.

So Martin Luther, the passionate preacher and roustabout theological debater and the public symbol of new alternatives beyond the church's control, had to be dealt with, with the efficiency that only force can provide. Early in 1520, the pope flexed his muscle, threatening Luther with excommunication. From his lodge in the mountains, where he was hunting wild boar, he issued a bull titled *Exsurge Domine* from its first Latin words: "Arise, O Lord, and drive out the boar that has invaded your vineyard. . . ." In a second bull, *Decet Romanum*, the pope formally excommunicated Luther. Excommunication, which formally removes a person from the church community, was often threatened and sometimes employed against heretics, public sinners, disobedient churchmen, and uncooperative or recalcitrant rulers. In an age when the church was involved in every sphere of the social world, excommunication imperiled the very livelihood and lives, not to say the immortal souls, of its recipients.

It took some time for the papal bull—the name used for such pronouncements—to arrive in Wittenberg. It didn't arrive until early in December 1520. It offered Luther time to submit but demanded that he recant or withdraw his criticisms. Given the way he had responded to prior directives, Luther's reaction was predictable. One morning, a group of students in tow, Luther went down to the bank of the River Elbe, which flows through Wittenberg, and burned the bull, along with a text of the canon law, which regulates the life of the church. Convicted of the power of the word, Luther wasn't going to submit to any other authority.

Whether he had learned of Luther's bonfire or not, in the winter of 1521, Pope Leo took the next step. The monk who had become a professor and stumbled into the vocation of a church reformer was now an excommunicant—barred from the sacraments of the church and deprived of its privileges and protections.

THE DIET OF WORMS

It was the tyranny of religion that led the framers of the American constitution to separate church and state. In medieval Europe, there was no such wall. Church and state were to work together for the overall welfare and unity of the people, the church overseeing spiritual matters, the state looking after the rest. But in fact, the two powers were constantly getting into each other's business. The pope claimed that since the spirit is superior to the flesh, he should have the last word, and he frequently got it. Kings and rulers were interested in their own independence and didn't mind giving the pope or his hierarchy a lump or two when the opportunity arose.

From the beginning, Luther's unintended reform had been mixed up in politics. Not having a local bishop to contend with, Frederick the Wise had been more than glad to look after church matters himself. He didn't know Luther personally; apparently they never met. The closest Luther got was through his friend Spalatin. But even in all the uproar, Frederick was still convinced that Luther deserved better than he had gotten—at bare minimum, a hearing. Frederick had enough standing and power to keep Luther safe, even after he had been excommunicated and outlawed.

For Charles V, the young, newly elected Holy Roman Emperor, Luther posed a problem. Charles had his own troubles with the pope. Fearing the power Charles already held, the papacy had opposed his election. At one point, later in the 1520s, relations between Rome and Charles became so difficult that Charles's troops sacked the city of Rome and briefly held the pope prisoner. While he had his convictions, Charles wasn't a very religious man. He was influenced also by the humanists. But as emperor he was very much concerned about the unity of Western Europe, since he himself ruled what is now Germany, parts of Eastern Europe, and Spain. He shared the medieval conviction that if the church were divided, Europe would be more vulnerable to attack by the Turks. The Reformation, exploding out of little Wittenberg and rapidly escalating, threatened both church and empire.

Charles had the power to do something about it. A Flemish speaker who had grown up in northern France, close to the Netherlands, he had a power base in the low countries. He also had a power base in Spain: Ferdinand and Isabella, who financed Columbus's voyage to the Americas, had been part of his family, and he became King Charles I of Spain. And as one of the Hapsburg family, he also had power in what is now Austria and Hungary, where his brother Ferdinand was in charge. That gave him three corners of a roughly shaped square; election as Holy Roman emperor had given him the fourth. Charles was one of the few Holy Roman emperors with power to rule that loose and unruly confederation of electors, princes, and local rulers. The story of his attempts to hold Europe together by quashing the burgeoning religious protest is basic to the whole Reformation.

Power draws animosity, of course, and Charles garnered plenty of it. Some of it came from the papacy, which sought to undercut him even while he understood himself to be protecting it. The French took a regular turn. Charles's Hapsburg family and the Valois, the royal family of France, fought a series of four wars during the Reformation. The Turks were the biggest threat, especially in Austria-Hungary. Later in the 1520s, they captured the cities of Buda and Pest and laid siege to Vienna. But the Germans also were their own challenge. Dividing and subdividing into smaller sovereignties—some as big as Saxony, some as small as independent cities—their local rulers guarded their powers zealously, trying to preserve as much independence as possible.

As a result, Charles had to deal with Frederick the Wise, just as he also had to deal with Frederick's successors in electoral Saxony. It would be decades before Charles could resort to force, and in the end that would fail. In 1521, Charles and Frederick negotiated. Even the famous humanist, Erasmus of Rotterdam, got involved. He minimized the conflict, insisting that Luther's only real offense had been to "attack the bellies of the monks." Frederick also tried to keep the matter in proportion, asking only that Luther be given something of a hearing.

When the chief rulers of the Holy Roman Empire were assembled—electors and princes, bishops and city representatives—their meetings were called diets. They could just as well have been called circuses. Medieval politicians were no different from the biblical or the modern ones—in fact, if anything, the contemporary ones have had to learn to be more circumspect. Whores came to town from all over Europe; beer, wine, and a new product, fortified wine or brandy, flowed freely; small fortunes were exchanged at the card tables. It was the boys' night out, an old-time convention.

Charles called a diet to assemble in April 1521 to meet in the southwestern German city of Worms (pronounced *Vorms*). It was and is a beautiful community, close to the grape-growing, wine-producing area. The diet was to deal with the controversy sparked by the early Reformation, settling the religious issue.

Because the pope had already pronounced his verdict on Luther, an open hearing was out of the question. In fact, the papal *nuncios*—the pope's diplomats, especially the papal ambassador Aleander—were determined that Luther should not even be given a chance to speak. There was some question, just as in the meeting with Cardinal Cajetan, about the wisdom of bringing Luther to the diet. But once more, there was a promise of safe conduct. Luther was expressly forbidden to publish any further theological tracts before the diet. Frederick and his advisors were confident that they could protect him. And so Luther went, traveling for two weeks across Germany by wagon, celebrated along the way as a German hero. He preached in churches, monasteries, and even fields all the way to Worms, where he was welcomed by thousands of people.

Frederick's advisors were determined to give Luther his day in the sun—a chance to speak. They advised him, in his first appearance before the diet, to ask for some time for consideration. According to the procedures, this guaranteed him a chance to make a statement. When he entered the assembly, amidst all of the rich dress, pomp and circumstance, he found a table containing copies of his publications. He was asked by a church official whether the books were his and, if so, whether he was willing to renounce them. Had he answered at that point, his hearing would have amounted to saying little more than a yes or no. So he spoke, softly but confidently—so quietly that some had difficulty hearing him, indicating that yes, the books were his but that God's word was at stake here, and he needed some time to consider. Some of his supporters nearby encouraged him, calling out Bible quotations. After consultations, the delay was granted. He was scheduled to appear before the diet the next afternoon.

It must have been a long night. Luther had visitors, though. He had gained enough support among the princes and other political leaders to win some encouragement from them. Frederick, even if he may still have had some questions about what his young professor was up to, also had allies supporting him. The visitors assured Luther of his safety, confident that there was enough backing to prevent the emperor from taking pre-emptive measures.

Diets, like conventions of any kind, take their own time. It was an unseasonably warm afternoon the next day; and Luther sat in his appointed place, awaiting his appearance in enforced inactivity. No doubt, he had plenty of time to think about what had brought him to this point and what would follow. Maybe he thought about the Apostle Paul, who had appeared before Roman authorities himself.

Finally, in the dimming darkness of early evening, Luther was brought before the diet—this time in a larger room lit with torches. It was full. Contrary to the usual custom, there were spectators. Luther wore his severe monastic haircut and black Augustinian monk's robe. He was wringing wet with perspiration. There he stood alone before the crowned heads of Germany, the emperor seated in the center of the room and the table of books standing in place. He was asked if he would renounce them. He started off diplomatically, begging the assembly's pardon for not knowing the proper manner for addressing such an august gathering because he was a monk.

Then like a good professor, Luther began to make some distinctions—now speaking boldly. Some of the books were expositions of Scripture, which even his enemies had commended for their quality. He couldn't renounce them without repudiating the biblical word, something he couldn't do. Some of them were articles he had written challenging papal abuse of power, abuses well enough known to require the criticism he had made. Still others were publications he had written in conflict with other professors, part of the duty of his vocation. He was willing to acknowledge that he had spoken excessively at some points, and he was willing to take responsibility for that, his only concession. Luther said that if it were proven that he was in error in anything he had written, he would gladly recant it and burn the books involved himself. But until then, he would have to stand fast.

By this time, the papal advisors were clearly bristling with impatience. No doubt, some of the politicians—eager for an evening meal and hungry for other adventures as well—were wondering about the necessity of all these distinctions. Then one of the emperor's men spoke, chastising Luther for his aggressiveness in attacking the papacy and once more, declaring the emperor's concern for the unity of the church. "Give us an answer without horns or teeth," he said, turning back to the original question.

Then Luther spoke directly and clearly some of the most famous words of the Reformation, words that once more echoed throughout Europe, cementing his standing as a German hero, installing him a permanent symbol of protest against the institutions of power:

> Unless I am convinced by the testimony of the Scripture or by clear reason (for I do not trust either in the pope or in the councils alone, since it is well known that they have often erred and contradicted themselves), I am bound by the Scriptures I have quoted, and my conscience is captive to the word of God. I cannot and I will not recant anything, since it is neither safe nor right to go against conscience. May God help me. Amen.

The hall erupted in an uproar. Luther had made his testimony before emperor, princes, and bishops, refusing to back down.

THE AFTERMATH

If someone at the Diet of Worms had asked him who he was, Luther could have answered in familiar terms: he was a miner's son who had become a monk and a priest, then a professor of biblical studies. At a deeper level, he was a sinner who had been so grasped by grace that his whole sense of himself in relation to God and others was captive by the word of God. But the forces that had coalesced around Martin Luther before the Diet of Worms had already made him something more than that: he represented protest against a church rife with abuses. He represented German discontent with Mediterranean dominance. And he represented the hopes of a people trying to come to terms with a new way of life. After the Diet of Worms, someone asked to describe Luther would say that he was more than all of that: a hero—or better, a prophet.

In fact, that is just how Luther came to be understood and to some extent, later in life, how he understood himself. The biblical parallels to his bold stance before the emperor reverberated to put Luther in line with Elijah and John the Baptist, with Isaiah or Jeremiah or Paul. He was not, as Melanchthon himself later said, an ordinary type of person. A symbol in the sixteenth century, for good or ill, Luther has retained the same status. He has been a symbol of the individual standing over and against society, of freedom of conscience, of the power of protest. His legacy—the heroic and the petty, the admirable and the not so—has become part of German, European, and world history, all symbolized by his appearance at the Diet of Worms.

At the time, however, Luther had an immediate problem: his safety. To Charles V, the papacy, and the forces allied around them, Luther and his teaching threatened a breach in the unity of Europe that had to be dealt with promptly. If Luther didn't know it, his friends and supporters did. They arranged for him to leave Worms on April 26 with an imperial escort. The party moved fast, traveling northeasterly toward Wittenberg. Along the way, Luther was captured by another party of horsemen, who took him away in what looked like a kidnapping. After standing center stage, under torchlight, in the midst of all the German powers, Luther disappeared on May 3 without a trace.

With Luther the person out of the picture, Charles V and his supporters—with the ardent backing of papal officials—dealt with Luther the symbol. Charles issued the Edict of Worms, condemning Luther and anyone who followed his way of thinking and declaring Luther an outlaw. If things had gone the way they usually do, that would have been the end of the story. Luther the monk, priest, and professor had become Luther the excommunicant and outlaw, now under imperial ban. But if symbols are risky, they also have a way of surviving—even against the best efforts of the powerful.

CHAPTER 5

THE CENTER DOES NOT HOLD

Martin Luther had been hauled out of obscurity and brought to the very center of German political life to testify before the emperor. One thing had led to another, the tension building by some seemingly inexorable force. Then, just when everyone was expecting a decisive climax, Luther disappeared. The politicians, hung over, nursing wounded pocketbooks, or full of pride in what had transpired, went home.

What would happen next? Charles V and the papal diplomats hoped that things would get back to normal. They had been around long enough to know that Luther was probably hidden away somewhere, but they must have been fairly confident that the Edict of Worms would be a sufficient threat to restrain his sympathizers. Perhaps Frederick the Wise shared this longing. He had gone out on a long limb for Luther, far enough to want some order restored.

In the meantime, other forces were pulling away at the center. Up to this point, the theological conflict between Luther and his Roman Catholic opponents had dominated attention. But Luther's writings had incited not only Roman legalism but also liberating license. A kind of spiritual enthusiasm was already building in both Wittenberg itself and on the German-Swiss border, threatening to overwhelm church order and cohesion.

Another party was yet to be heard from, as well: Renaissance humanism. In fact, northern European humanists had their own visions of church reform. Erasmus, the most important of them, had weighed in with Luther at Worms, but he was apprehensive about some of Luther's arguments. Trouble was brewing there. The southwest German and Swiss theologians, many of them Erasmus's students, were beginning to complain about Luther's views on the Lord's Supper.

Beyond all the political and theological machinations, another group—restive and complaining—was eager to improve their situation, and not willing to wait much longer. They were watching their sons and daughters move off to the cities, wondering what was next for them. And they were ready to take matters into their own hands. The farmers or peasants, on the edge of revolt, would soon get pulled over the edge.

It looked as if all hell was going to break loose. And in fact, it did. Between 1521 and 1527, the center did not hold—political, religious, and social change mushroomed until it appeared that chaos had taken over.

IN THE REGION OF THE BIRDS

Luther's kidnapping after the Diet of Worms was arranged not by bandits or papal or imperial agents but by Frederick the Wise. Carrying with him only the Hebrew Scriptures and Erasmus's recent Greek edition of the New Testament, Luther was taken, circuitously, in a trip that lasted several days, to a castle up the mountain from Eisenach in eastern Germany—the Wartburg. There he was put into a room, and he didn't begin to move around the grounds more freely until his monastic haircut and beard had grown out. His true identity hidden, he was known there as Sir George, a knight down on his luck—just the type to take up temporary residence in a castle that had fallen into some disrepair.

Later, the Wartburg became more of a landmark. Luther lent it some fame. Now it is a tourist attraction. Visitors are shown a carefully maintained mark on the wall, suitably faded, where Luther's inkwell is supposed to have hit when he flung it at the devil, who was taunting him.

Luther did have some real struggles at the Wartburg. The dread and anxiety from his earlier years returned, in force. It is hardly surprising. Restless, driven, used to working up to seventy-two hours at a time, then falling into bed exhausted, only to rise and go again, Luther was not accustomed to leisure. Time and again in the past, his anxieties had arisen out of enforced inactivity and silence.

There were other sources of anxiety, as well. The pope and the emperor had stripped Luther of all the usual protections. Even though Frederick was continuing to shelter him, he was still under threat. Once, with time on his hands, he went hunting with some of the others at the Wartburg. A rabbit, panicked by the dogs in close pursuit, ran right up Luther's sleeve. The dogs bit right through it, killing the rabbit and reminding Luther of himself, pursued by the papists.

Another source of Luther's troubled state was the devil. While the idea of the devil seems mythological today, people in Luther's time readily believed in the personification of evil. They were well-acquainted with the unpredictable forces at the dark edges of human experience.

For Luther, a person of faith, the real conflict was the devilish temptation to self-doubt. Thinking of Noah building the ark while his neighbors went about business as usual, he wondered, "Am I the only one who knows this?" It was his father's question, all over again. "Is it God or the devil? Is this faith or an illusion? Have I really heard God speaking in the word and the sacraments, or is it just my own self?" At one point, he became so incapacitated by his despair that for more than a week he could hardly move, let alone work.

Yet for all of his criticism of salvation by good works, it was work that saved him—at least from the *ennui* that beset him. Luther went back to his writing and in the next ten months produced some of his most important work. He finished a commentary on the Magnificat, the Virgin Mary's wonderful song on learning that she would be the mother of Jesus—a classical statement of Luther's faith. And he went to work on two other projects that would be among his most lasting contributions.

One was the Postil, a series of sermons on the Gospel texts assigned for preaching throughout the church year. Over the centuries, many such series had been published. Luther knew some of them, and he made arrangements to get a hold of the traditional lectionary—the schedule of texts. He never preached the sermons he wrote. They are more like sermon starters, reflections on the texts to help both preachers and hearers think through the texts. They have long been considered among the very best of Luther's writings. The Postil has fired some renewal movements of its own, in places as far apart as northern Scandinavia and Madagascar.

The other project was longer term. Philip Melanchthon had been helping Luther with his Greek; Luther also knew enough Hebrew to work with it carefully. Still, he was not as good a translator as some others, such as Melanchthon himself or some of the Hebrew teachers. But at the Wartburg, Luther had both the time and the texts. He went to work on the New Testament, translating the whole work from Greek to German in amazing time, approximately eleven weeks. When he ran into trouble with the Greek, he did what Erasmus himself had done in producing his Greek edition: he used Jerome's Latin translation, which for more than a millennium had been the official Roman Catholic text of the Bible. He also began his translation of the Old Testament, a draft of which he finished the following year. Eventually, he translated the New Testament in its entirety three times, the Old Testament twice. What he lacked in expertise in the original languages, he more than made up for with his ear for the language of the home and the streets. His translation became, until well into the twentieth century, the German Bible, deeply influencing the development of the German language, giving him the same place in German that Shakespeare and the translators of the King James Version have had in English. Culturally, it may have been his greatest achievement of all.

Luther arrived at the Wartburg in early May of 1521. In September he went to work on the New Testament. By December, he was looking for ways to break out of his confinement. Troubles in Wittenberg were drawing him back. Frederick and Spalatin were still not sure of his safety. In a secret trip back, Luther stopped by a tavern incognito—his long hair and beard protected his identity—and listened to the patrons speculating about where he might be. Melanchthon couldn't restrain the chaos getting loose in Wittenberg itself. In the end, Luther felt compelled to return to Wittenberg and to the many controversies and reforms occasioned by his writings.

THE RADICALS

With Luther's bold questioning of church practices, the meaning of the Mass, and even monastic vows, there was bound to be someone who believed that all the normal restraints had been abolished. That someone was Andreas Bodenstein von Carlstadt, one of Luther's colleagues on the Wittenberg faculty. With several doctorates and a fine mind, Carlstadt was as knowledgeable as anyone. But his knowledge didn't necessarily guarantee his common sense. Initially opposed to Luther's breakthrough, he eventually accepted it and then took Luther's way of thinking to what Carlstadt thought was its logical conclusion. In the process, he became a key leader in what has come to be called "the Radical Reformation."

Carlstadt's point of departure was the power of the Holy Spirit. Luther was convinced that the Spirit uses external means—the word preached by another person, the sacraments administered—to accomplish its purposes. Carlstadt was convinced that the Spirit spoke directly to people apart from the Bible. Carlstadt wandered the streets of Wittenberg in his professor's robes, asking illiterate peasants to give him the spiritual interpretation of God's word. That isn't all bad—it doesn't take a doctor's degree to understand the Scripture. But not everything that pops into a pious head is the biblical word, either. Some check is needed, just the point Carlstadt resisted.

During Luther's absence Melanchthon had vacillated about Carstadt's innovations, alternatively conceding to Carlstadt and then taking a heavy hand. It seemed as though the freedom unleashed by Luther's reforms was out of control. Disputes arose over reforms to the Mass, confession, the vows of the monks, and whether "life in the Spirit" entailed any rules at all.

When Luther returned, he took the lead once more, preaching a series of sermons in March 1522. He had the following to settle things, which is exactly what he did. He preached about the law, the Ten Commandments, and the need for faith to be active in love. He reined in some innovations. Melanchthon felt repudiated. For the next five years, the friendship between him and Luther hung in suspension. It was restored only when Luther cared for Philip and Barbara Melanchthon in the loss of their child. But the Wittenberg reformation was put back on course—Luther had restored a more traditional practice, emphasizing preaching and the sacraments.

Carlstadt left Wittenberg to wander through Germany, gathering followers for his more radical vision of the Christian faith. Some of his friends and associates allied themselves with the forces that came to a head in the Peasants' War in 1525. Other influences also fed in from Switzerland to power the Radical or Left-wing Reformation, as it is also called. Some of the radicals were called Anabaptists from their practice of rebaptizing adults—they practiced what they called "believer's baptism," convinced that children cannot be validly baptized. Generally, they withdrew from public life to form "societies of the just"—separate communities of the truly converted. Hutterites, Mennonites, and Baptists trace their origins to this movement. Other radicals have been called "evangelical spiritualists"—they rejected all church structures, regarding them as inherently evil, the church being an invisible fellowship of the saints. Still another small group has been named "anti-trinitarian rationalists." For them, the real problem with the church was the doctrine of the trinity, which should be rejected in favor of simple faith in Jesus. Strasbourg, on the German-French border, and the city of Muenster became famous havens for the radical reformers. Though driven underground by Roman Catholic authorities and also by those supporting Luther, the radicals became another force at large in the chaos of the early Reformation.

THE HUMANISTS

Luther had learned a lot from the humanists. Becoming acquainted with humanism during his Erfurt days, he had been impressed particularly by the humanist love of ancient Greek and Latin literature. He relished Aesop's fables, for example, throughout his life. And he enjoyed Cicero, the great Roman orator. Luther once said that if anyone could be saved apart from Christ, he hoped Cicero would be included. But his biblical studies, even if they were driven by humanistic ideals of working directly with ancient sources, led him to be much more concerned about God's justifying promise than manners and morals, the preoccupations of the typical northern European humanists that he knew.

Erasmus of Rotterdam, the premier intellectual in late fifteenth- and sixteenth-century Europe, was the leader of the humanists. The illegitimate son of a Dutch priest and a physician's daughter, Erasmus had been ordained a priest and then secured some endowments that enabled him to move around Europe's universities, teaching at several of them, especially in Basel, Switzerland. Witty and sarcastic, he had been a guest at some of the great tables of Europe and consulted on the issues of the day. He embodied the humanists' high regard for classical Greek and Roman culture, low tolerance for corruption and dogmatism, and admiration for the dignity and worth of being human.

Above all, he was a linguist, styling himself after St. Jerome, the great translator of the early church. He occasionally published books, including some light satires. But generally he maintained his influence through letters. Some twenty-eight volumes of his correspondence have been collected.

Through the early years of the Reformation, Erasmus had given Luther some vital support. Erasmus's Greek New Testament, published while he was in Basel, was the basis of Luther's translation into German. But Erasmus was becoming increasingly concerned about what he took to be Luther's doctrinaire pronouncements on issues Erasmus considered much more complex and open-ended. The matter that bothered Erasmus the most was Luther's denial of the freedom of the human will, an issue that had come up in the *Heidelberg Disputation* and other of Luther's writings. At Heidelberg, Luther had argued that "freedom of the will, after the fall, exists in name only"—a statement that had been quoted against Luther in the pope's bull of condemnation. So in 1524, Erasmus wrote his *On the Freedom of the Will*, challenging both the surety with which Luther spoke and the conclusions he drew.

Luther's disagreements with Erasmus were a terrible embarrassment to Melanchthon, himself an ardent humanist. He had had his own difficulties with Luther's apparently authoritarian, even arrogant, manner of speaking, especially upon Luther's return to Wittenberg. Yet even if their friendship was strained, he had stuck with Luther and his theological point of view. But now Luther, temperamental and self-assured, had gotten himself into a clash with the mind of the century—a man to whom Melanchthon also felt himself deeply indebted. Worse yet, the odds hardly looked even.

Luther also knew the odds. As aware of Erasmus's reputation as anyone, he had appreciated and respected him as a senior colleague even while being occasionally critical of him. But he was also convinced that Erasmus had raised the fundamental issue: how much a person is capable of in relation to God. "You alone have not bothered me with trifles," Luther acknowledged to Erasmus, when he wrote his reply in what became the greatest theological debate of the Lutheran Reformation.

In some ways, the issue between Luther and Erasmus was as much personal as it was theological. Erasmus—refined, skeptical, absorbed in issues of style and personal deportment—was something of a spectator, living one step removed from the fray, given to sarcastic barbs about the stupidities and inanities of other people. In contrast, Luther was aggressive if not bold, free with himself, sure of his convictions, casual about appearances, a fully engaged participant in life, and, in matters other than controversy, inclined to be overly generous. Erasmus looked at life from the top down; Luther from the bottom up.

Later on, when Luther looked back over his writings, nearly 150 large volumes, he singled out his reply to Erasmus, *The Bondage of the Will*, as one of his few works worthy of preservation. It is a masterpiece of polemic, difficult to read because of Luther's close attention to Erasmus's points and some of the complexities of the argument but worth all the labor.

Luther's two most important arguments in *The Bondage of the Will* involve the clarity of the Bible and the nature of freedom. On the first, Erasmus had argued that the Bible is ambiguous and that because different interpretations are possible an authoritative teaching office is needed to determine which interpreter is accurate. Luther argued that the overall message of Scripture is summed up in Christ's death and resurrection, that read in this way the overall message of Scripture is crystal clear and that therefore the word of God stands alone—without any necessary props from the church. Where individual passages remain obscure, they can be clarified by Scripture itself. Read with faith, Scripture interprets Scripture.

On the nature of freedom, the second issue, Luther made two arguments about the bound will. One grows out of John 8, "anyone who commits sin is a slave of sin." While people do have some freedom of choice in matters that reason can comprehend—what clothes to wear, political decisions, and the like—in matters above us, that is in relation to God, sin holds us captive. It works in the appetites, in the desires of the heart, binding the self to the self, so that we are caught in our own traps. Like a shy person attempting to be outgoing, we find that our effort backfires, leaving us even more self-conscious than before and compounding our anxiety. Left alone, we have no way out: our freedom is a delusion. Luther's other argument comes from the omnipotence of God. Working with classical theological distinctions concerning the nature of God, Luther argues that if God is God, God is free, and for that reason, the creatures God has made cannot be.

Luther measured every word, calculating even the jokes for their effect. Erasmus was stunned. Erasmus's *On the Freedom of the Will* is short and sweet, stylistically wrought—"manure in silver dishes," Luther called it. By contrast, for all of its elaborate reasoning, humor, and thoroughgoing biblical and theological argumentation, Luther's *Bondage of the Will* is as pointed as an arrow. Erasmus spent the next several years writing a reply that came to more than seven hundred pages—so large and complex that one contemporary student of the debate claims to be the only person in recent centuries to have read it. Luther won the battle, even if in the end he lost the war. Erasmus's more facile understanding of the free will, even if it is no longer associated with his name, became a keystone for modern life, while Luther's deeper probes into the troubled character of human freedom are often ignored.

If Erasmus's attack wasn't enough—further evidence of the chaos breaking out around him—there were some other humanists on Luther's trail, this time with an issue concerning the Mass, or as Luther called it, the Lord's Supper. The medieval Catholic understanding of the Mass turned on the doctrine of transubstantiation, a thirteenth-century teaching crystallizing previous convictions of the church that the bread and wine in the sacrament become the real body and blood of Jesus Christ. This change undergirds the value of the church's offering. It also bolsters the authority of the hierarchy because the priest alone, through ordination by his bishop, is authorized to present the sacrifice and obtain grace for further distribution.

Luther attacked the sacrifice of the Mass in his own way. The Lord's Supper is not a sacrifice but a sacrament. The church is not the agent at work; God is, distributing the benefits of Christ's death and resurrection to those who eat and drink. For this reason, though he dismissed the doctrine of transubstantiation as an unnecessary explanation of what happens under Christ's promise, Luther also insisted that the real body and blood of Christ Jesus are "in, with, and under" the bread and the wine.

Humanist theologians in southwest Germany and Switzerland, many of whom had studied with Erasmus, took a different tack. They were convinced, like Luther, that the sacrifice of the Mass was the central element in the sacramental system and in medieval Catholic abuses. But they wanted to correct the situation by severing the identity of the bread and wine from Christ's actual body and blood. So, following another tradition that appears in the history of the church, they used various words to describe the relationship between Christ and the elements—the blood and wine represent, symbolize, or exhibit Christ's body and blood to the faithful. They accused Luther and his Wittenbergers, among other things, of not going far enough, of perpetuating the superstition of transubstantiation. Luther in turn accused the southwest Germans and Swiss of making Christ's presence dependent on the faith of the believers.

There are several names associated with this conflict. The best known is Ulrich Zwingli, the city pastor in Zurich who also had some influence in the Radical Reformation. A Swiss patriot who also served as a military chaplain, Zwingli was nearly the same age as Luther and supported him early in the Reformation, before the conflict over the sacrament. Another was Martin Bucer, who heard Luther at Heidelberg and later on became pastor in the city of Strasbourg. Still a third was a friend of Melanchthon's who had Latinized his name to Oecolampadius.

Like many other conflicts in the Reformation, this one was complicated by German politics. Southwest Germany, down to the Swiss border, has been called the Upper Rhine region, for the river that flows through it. Upper Rhine and Saxon Germans spoke a different dialect, and linguistic and old cultural tensions between the regions figured in the feud. Once more, things seemed to be falling further apart, and on a critically important matter, the sacrament itself.

THE PEASANTS' WAR

If, to this point, chaos had manifested itself in a helter-skelter of theological parties pulling away from the center, another force at work would soon make the chaos altogether too real. Luther's early support from the peasants, tradespeople, and migrants to the cities had been strong and important. They were Luther's audience, and they heard him gladly. He was sympathetic to their grievances, as they were to his message of freedom from oppressive authorities. In 1525 those forces exploded in one of the most dramatic incidents of the Reformation, the Peasants' War. Once more, Luther was involved up to his ears. Once more, his language was a powerful factor, and again it got away from him, leaving him with a seemingly permanent blot on his reputation.

The great voyages of discovery in the fourteenth, fifteenth, and sixteenth centuries didn't have much apparent direct effect in the remote regions of Germany. Christopher Columbus, Vasco de Gama, Ponce de Leon, and others were Italian, Portuguese, or Spanish. Luther had heard rumors of Columbus's discoveries, but those voyages had been funded by the Mediterranean business community for financial reasons. The explorers were opening trade routes, bringing back spices and other goods. And just as they excited new appetites, they also required cash.

The lords and nobles, the upper class in Germany, were eager to get into the new economy. But for several centuries, they had been bound together with their workers—the peasants—in a system of mutual dependence that kept things relatively in balance. In the feudal system, the lords needed the peasants to produce their crops; the workers required the lords both for property and protection. It worked by barter, goods and produce being traded back and forth, with labor keeping up the supply. If the lords were to take advantage of new luxuries flowing across the Alps from Italy or from Spain and Portugal, they were going to have to get beyond the barter system and raise some cash. They did so by putting the squeeze on the farmers—by charging rents, by assessing fees on common pastures and firewood, and by charging for water rights, hunting, and fishing.

The lords had the advantage, of course. They not only owned the property but also had prior standing with the law. And they used it, putting more and more pressure on the peasants. The peasants, like primary producers in any economic chain, had literally nowhere to turn. It was pay or leave, which many of them did.

Luther was no economist and no capitalist, either. He was dead set against collecting interest on loans, citing good biblical evidence in his favor. He once wrote that anything that a person has that is not used to serve the neighbor is, in fact, stolen. But like everyone else, he knew the peasants' complaints. If he needed reminding, they were published in a document called *The Twelve Articles* in the spring of 1525. In fact, he published an article of his own, *An Admonition to Peace,* supporting the peasants and urging negotiations between them and the princes and lords, whom he said would otherwise get what they deserved.

By the time Luther's pamphlet reached the public, the peasants had already done what he anticipated and feared. Armed with pikes and forks, the implements of work, they went after the lords to exact repayment for the oppression they had endured. Characteristically, Luther described what happened in biblical language, recalling images of Noah's flood; it was as though the bowels of the earth had opened, chaos spilling all over. With things falling apart all around him and now chaos churning through the streets and fields, Luther wrote against the peasants in harsh and dramatic terms, urging the lords to "stab, slay, and smite" those responsible for the insurrection.

Once again, Luther had trouble with his timing, which complicated his verbal excesses even further. His pamphlet, *Against the Robbing and Murdering Hordes of Peasants,* appeared just as the lords were doing exactly what Luther had exhorted them to do, and more. The peasants, disorganized, lacking discipline and trained leadership, were quickly overcome. When the lords regained the advantage, they kept it, wreaking a vengeance that put the peasants' cause back—by some estimates— up to one hundred fifty years. An estimated one hundred thousand peasants died.

Luther's sympathy for the peasants had been overwhelmed by his strong sense of the legitimacy of "temporal" or political authority. Perhaps, if he had been someone else, he would have been wise enough to admit his mistake. He had, after all, by this time written against both the lords and the peasants. But what made him so powerful in standing in the face of papal and imperial opposition also made it impossible for him to back down, even when he needed to do so. He published a third writing, *On the Harsh Book against the Peasants,* seeking to justify his earlier writing. Understandably, he lost the support of the peasants. The incident has been marked against him ever since. Though he himself had been a fearless religious rebel, his fear of chaos had led him to oppose the peasant rebels, and his stubbornness would not allow him to concede that he had inflamed the situation further.

CHAPTER 6

LUTHER AT HOME:
REFUGE FROM CHAOS

When Luther returned from the Wartburg in 1522, he moved back into the Augustinian monastery, the Black Cloister, and took up where he had left off. There was a difference. As one monk after another decided to leave monastic life to seek a secular vocation—a process that had started when Luther was away—the building had emptied out. Before long, Luther and another monk, Jerome, were the last left.

With all of the new problems emerging, Luther also returned to a more familiar front—the ongoing conflict with Rome. On that front, the issue was still whether and how a person is saved or made right or "justified" by faith. In the early 1520s, Luther wrote an important statement on justification by faith. Typically, it came out of a conflict, this one with a Louvain theologian named Latomus. Along with the commentaries on Paul's letters, *Against Latomus* is one of Luther's most helpful considerations of the topic.

Surprisingly, as crucial as the doctrine was in the Reformation, Luther didn't ever write a treatise devoted to justification by faith alone as its exclusive topic. At one point, later in his life, he did talk about such a project. He said it wasn't going to be so much an article or book as a rhapsody, a song of praise and thanksgiving.

Luther thought about justification by faith at two levels. At one level, it is closely related to one of Luther's original goals in what became the Reformation: to improve preaching. In his mind, theology or doctrine isn't an end in itself. Rather, it is a way of thinking about the word that has been heard so that it can be spoken again and thereby handed on to another. At this level, the doctrine of justification functions like a grammar that describes how the Gospel word is to be spoken. As a kind of grammar, the doctrine of justification states that when Christ is preached, he is to be presented as the one in whom God is acting. As in the Gospels, Christ is the one who is always working—healing, freeing, forgiving sinners, raising the dead. The grammar of justification holds that Christ's gifts and benefits are to be handed over to the people listening, so that they benefit by what he does. Because Christ is the one at work in the word, his gifts are to be given unconditionally here and now—without further mediation or qualification.

At another level, the doctrine of justification had occupied Luther in both his sermon on *Two Kinds of Righteousness* and *The Freedom of a Christian*. Words like *justice* and *righteousness*, in their original sense, describe a relationship in which things are properly aligned, in their place, true to their purpose—right in the deepest meaning of the word. In Luther's way of thinking, this relationship wasn't a moral or legal quality that could be achieved—that, he thought, was precisely the problem. When sinners try to make themselves righteous, instead of "dying" to their old selves, the old self takes charge of trying to make the new being. In Luther's view, the inevitable result will be pride or despair, that is, self-righteousness in the worst sense or the desperate conviction that one can never be righteous before God. For Luther, "earning" righteousness was futile in every sense.

Rather, Luther's experience and study showed him the righteousness that God creates in us through Christ is personal and relational. It is like the deep friendship that often develops between a parent and an adult child. They so love and trust one another that there is no question of having to conform to any legal requirements. So, in a beautiful image, Luther says that when Christ justifies, he restores a person—his people—to the point "from which Adam fell." Or again, he makes people "what Adam and Eve were meant to be, only better"—better not in a moral or legal sense but better in that faith has taken hold, so that they turn to God naturally, confidently, expectantly, rejoicing in God's bare naked goodness.

Luther's question during the early 1520s was how this righteousness works out in the tribulations and joys of everyday life. Thinking about this issue, he wrote several essays, among them *The Judgment of Martin Luther on Monastic Vows*. In the process, he worked out one of his most important teachings, the doctrine of vocation. A person does not become a believer by going away to a monastery and trying to achieve a righteousness of his or her own—that is the old legal way of thinking. Rather, as God justifies in Christ, God calls us into the vocations of everyday life: into families, where children are born and shaped for life; into work, where the service of neighbor commonly happens; into the community through citizenship, where people contribute together to the common good; into the church, where people gather to hear the word, receive the sacraments, and care for one another.

Each of these relationships involves a cross. They are the points where the old Adam or the old Eve meets with decisive defeat, no matter how strenuous our efforts. The struggles of family life, the drudgery of work, the inevitable contradictions of community life, the conflicts of the church bring with them their own forms of loss. Here sinners die, not because they seek or desire it, but because of the shape that these relationships take in a sin-driven world. But here, too, in these very relationships the power of the resurrection manifests itself—in the joy of seeing a child come to maturity, in the satisfaction of a job well done, in the gifts bestowed by citizenship, in the delights of life shared under the word in the church.

As Luther himself put it in a 1522 essay, *The Estate of Marriage*, with a characteristically sharp edge and bubbling humor:

> Along comes the clever harlot, namely natural reason, looks at married life, turns up her nose, and says: Why must I rock the baby, wash its diapers, change its bed, smell its odor, heal its rash, take care of this and take care of that, do this and do that? It is better to remain single and live a quiet and carefree life. I will become a priest or a nun and tell my children to do the same.
>
> But what does the Christian faith say? The father opens his eyes, looks at these lowly, distasteful and despised things and knows that they are adorned with divine approval as with the most precious gold and silver. God, with his angels and creatures, will smile—not because diapers are washed, but because it is done in faith.

This teaching on vocation, a correlate of justification by faith and a deep affirmation of the worth and purpose of daily life, became one of the most powerful appeals in Luther's Reformation. With the doctrine of justification, he attacked the religiosity that had permeated the late medieval period as the church had sought to dominate every aspect of life. As he saw it, such religion—the self-seeking, heaven-storming attempt to fulfill the law—was original sin itself. With the doctrine of vocation, he showed the value and dignity, the ultimate power of God's meeting the faithful in everyday life. For a people forced off the land where their families had lived for generations, who were driven into the cities to find new forms of work, who were taking on new roles as more independent citizens and church members, both teachings brought the word of God joyfully home.

LORD KATIE

Then what about Luther himself? He knew how to work—he had learned it at home and labored unceasingly since then. Even exhausted, he would drag himself out of his unchanged, sweat-encrusted straw bed and toil for days before falling into it again. Even losing civil protections, he knew full well both the duties and joys of citizenship. And he spent virtually every waking moment thinking about the church and its message. But there is something peculiar about a monk writing an essay like *The Estate of Marriage* and discoursing on diapers. And his *Judgment on Monastic Vows* might have rung a little hollow, too, especially when he was among the last to live in his own monastery. Something was going to have to change, even if he had no idea how, and it did.

At that point, the person who changed Luther's situation and his whole life most dramatically was a nun living in a convent in the territory of Duke George of Saxony, one of Luther's most ardent enemies. Blended families, in which father and mother bring together children from previous marriages, have always been challenging. Katherine von Bora's father had apparently decided to lower the risk. When he remarried, he placed her, a ten-year-old, in a Cistercian convent with nuns—a common practice. She accepted the arrangement, at least for the time being; and when she was sixteen, she took her vows.

But in the early 1520s, several factors—Luther's arguments included—came together and led people out of the monasteries and convents. In fact, another emptying like this would not occur until the twentieth century. Katherine von Bora wanted out, as did eight other nuns at Nimmschen, where she lived. It was a risky prospect, at several levels. Vows had to be broken and family disapproval met. Duke George was more than willing to use force to keep the monks and nuns in place. Given the treatment of women in the sixteenth century, their prospects out of the convent were not certain. There was the possibility of marriage, though eligible males might not be enamored of a former nun. Failing that, the likelihood was indenture to another family—or prostitution.

Katherine von Bora was not exactly what is now called risk-averse. Strong, independent, possessed of a mind of her own, she was ready to take the consequences. In 1523, she and her sisters contacted Luther, asking for help. He made arrangements with a man who delivered pickled herring to the convent to take them out in his barrels. They arrived in Wittenberg, eager to find new lives.

Luther had other things on his mind, enough so that he may not have especially welcomed a calling as a marriage broker, but he had some responsibility to the women. He handled it successfully with all of them except Katherine von Bora, even though she was apparently attractive enough. At one point, there had been some prospect with a nobleman that didn't work out. At another time, Luther had arranged a match for her with a younger man—this time, family objections took him in a different direction. It was into the spring of 1525, and still there was no marriage. When Luther tried to marry her off to an older man in the community, a Dr. Glatz, Katherine von Bora herself objected. Then, when Luther's friend and colleague, Nicholas von Amsdorf, with some impatience, asked whom she would have, Katherine answered either him or Dr. Luther.

Did Luther break with the church specifically in order to marry? He did acknowledge to a noblewoman who had encouraged him to marry that he was not a "sexless stone." Like many celibate monks and priests, he had had his own frustrations. But it was seven or eight years after the beginning of the Reformation, four years since his excommunication. He had said in 1522, when he first heard of Wittenberg monks marrying, "No one is going to put a wife on me." For a while Katherine von Bora apparently stayed at the Black Cloister. With some thirty vacant monastic cells, there was plenty of room. A charge directed to Katherine von Bora in a letter a year later was that they had lived together.

Other factors were at work. Maybe one of them was Luther's own thinking about vocation. Encouraging others in the callings of everyday life, perhaps he realized that he had to consider family responsibilities himself. Certainly another one was old Hans, Luther's father. He and Margarethe both wanted grandchildren.

One thing is sure: love had nothing to do with it, at least not in the beginning. In the sixteenth century, as now in many parts of the world, people generally did not look for a mate, fall in love, and then get married. Marriages were most often arranged, just as Luther himself had made arrangements for others. Couples married first and then came to love one another, if they were going to—and that is just what happened between Martin and Katie.

Whatever the reason, Luther decided to take his one remaining escaped nun at her word—whether she was serious or not. In June 1525, an agreement was struck, the betrothal was announced, and Dr. Martin Luther—forty-two-year-old monk, professor, priest, reformer, and outlaw—and Katherine von Bora, formerly a sister at Nimmschen, were united in holy matrimony on June 13. Though they were surely aware of the scandal involved, Hans and Margarethe were right there, beaming.

As their years together unfolded, Katherine von Bora or "Katie, my rib," as Luther often called her, must have wondered about what she had gotten herself into with such a partner. Monasteries are not a school for marriage. Luther did mend his own clothes, a practice he had learned in the cloister, but he wasn't above using the kids' underwear when he was looking for material for patches. He was compulsively generous, convinced that anything that he considered extra—whether cash or a gift provided by some admirer—was meant to be passed on, even as his new wife was trying to make ends meet on his professor's salary. Once he wrote to a friend who was marrying, saying that he was sending along a vase that had been given to him. In a postscript he adds that he couldn't provide the vase because Katie had hidden it.

Then, too, Luther continued to have his struggles with despair, withdrawing into his study for days at a time. Katie may not have taken it as a compliment when he wrote to a friend that admiring Katie's backside was the perfect antidote. Once when the bleakness was upon him and he had gone to his office, she had the door removed and forced him out. Another time, according to legend, Luther emerged to find his wife and children all dressed in black. He asked who had died.

"God has died," Katherine von Bora replied.

"This is impossible," Luther said. "God cannot die."

"Then why are you behaving as though God were dead?" she challenged him.

But Katherine von Bora managed, and more than that. She accepted the traditional duties of a wife, managing the household and more. The elector gave the two of them the Black Cloister as a residence. In addition to providing housing for the family, it became something of a dorm; Katherine von Bora complained regularly about the students' disregard for the fees she charged. It was also a hospital. With the knowledge she had gained of medical treatments in the convent, Katherine von Bora regularly cared for the sick, to the point where their son Paul, who became a physician himself, called her more than half a doctor. The Black Cloister was also a hotel, guests from all over Europe

Luther in Erfurt monastery
Martin Luther: Joseph Fiennes / Photo: Rolf von der Heydt
Director: Eric Till / DOP: Robert Fraisse
Luther © 2003 NFP teleart in cooperation with Thrivent Financial for Lutherans

Luther forgets his lines
Martin Luther: Joseph Fiennes / Photo: Rolf von der Heydt
Director: Eric Till / DOP: Robert Fraisse
Luther © 2003 NFP teleart in cooperation with Thrivent Financial for Lutherans

A street in Rome as Julius rides by
Photo: Rolf von der Heydt
Director: Eric Till / DOP: Robert Fraisse
Luther © 2003 NFP teleart in cooperation with Thrivent Financial for Lutherans

Luther shares doubts with Staupitz
Martin Luther: Joseph Fiennes / Staupitz: Bruno Ganz
Photo: Rolf von der Heydt / Director: Eric Till / DOP: Robert Fraisse
Luther © 2003 NFP teleart in cooperation with Thrivent Financial for Lutherans

Pope Leo is crowned
Pope Leo X: Uwe Ochsenknecht / Photo: Rolf von der Heydt
Director: Eric Till / DOP: Robert Fraisse
Luther © 2003 NFP teleart in cooperation with Thrivent Financial for Lutherans

Morality play in Wittenberg
Photo: Rolf von der Heydt
Director: Eric Till / DOP: Robert Fraisse
Luther © 2003 NFP teleart in cooperation with Thrivent Financial for Lutherans

Pope Leo discusses the restoration of St. Peter's
Pope Leo X: Uwe Ochsenknecht / Aleander: Jonathan Firth / Cardinal Cajetan: Mathieu Carriè
Photo: Rolf von der Heydt / Director: Eric Till / DOP: Robert Fraisse
Luther © 2003 NFP teleart in cooperation with Thrivent Financial for Lutherans

Tetzel speaks to the crowd
Tetzel: Alfred Molina / Photo: Rolf von der Heydt
Director: Eric Till / DOP: Robert Fraisse
Luther © 2003 NFP teleart in cooperation with Thrivent Financial for Lutherans

Frederick pays for a rose and abandons relics
Frederick the Wise: Sir Peter Ustinov / Spalatin: Benjamin Sadler
Photo: Rolf von der Heydt / Director: Eric Till / DOP: Robert Fraisse
Luther © 2003 NFP teleart in cooperation with Thrivent Financial for Lutherans

Luther burns a papal bull
Martin Luther: Joseph Fiennes / Photo: Rolf von der Heydt
Director: Eric Till / DOP: Robert Fraisse
Luther © 2003 NFP teleart in cooperation with Thrivent Financial for Lutherans

Frederick speaks with Charles V
Frederick the Wise: Sir Peter Ustinov / Aleander: Jonathan Firth / Spalatin: Benjamin Sadler
Charles V: Torben Liebrecht / Photo: Rolf von der Heydt / Director: Eric Till / DOP: Robert Fra
Luther © 2003 NFP teleart in cooperation with Thrivent Financial for Lutherans

von der Eck confronts Luther with charges
Martin Luther: Joseph Fiennes / von der Eck: Christopher Buchholz / Aleander: Jonathan Firt
Charles V: Torben Liebrecht / Photo: Rolf von der Heydt / Director: Eric Till / DOP: Robert Fra
Luther © 2003 NFP teleart in cooperation with Thrivent Financial for Lutherans

Luther listens to von der Eck
Martin Luther: Joseph Fiennes / Photo: Rolf von der Heydt
Director: Eric Till / DOP: Robert Fraisse
Luther © 2003 NFP teleart in cooperation with Thrivent Financial for Lutherans

Luther is granted a day to consider the charges
Martin Luther: Joseph Fiennes / Photo: Rolf von der Heydt
Director: Eric Till / DOP: Robert Fraisse`
Luther © 2003 NFP teleart in cooperation with Thrivent Financial for Lutherans

Luther and Katie teach children from the Bible
Martin Luther: Joseph Fiennes / Katie: Claire Cox
Photo: Rolf von der Heydt / Director: Eric Till / DOP: Robert Fraisse
Luther © 2003 NFP teleart in cooperation with Thrivent Financial for Lutherans

Emperor Charles at Augsburg
Charles V: Torben Liebrecht / Photo: Rolf von der Heydt
Director: Eric Till / DOP: Robert Fraisse
Luther © 2003 NFP teleart in cooperation with Thrivent Financial for Lutherans

dropping in to stay for unpredictable periods. In fact, when Johann Agricola moved back to Wittenberg to teach, Luther invited him and his wife Elsa to move in for awhile. They had nine children and stayed for several months. The old monastery also became a part-time orphanage. Luther occasionally brought home whole families of children in need of care.

To handle all of this, Katherine von Bora required some help. The Luthers hired some servants, but Katie's aunt, whom the children came to know as "Mumme Lena," also moved in and was much beloved.

Obtaining enough food and drink for such a household was a constant issue. They eventually bought a large vegetable garden plot and a fish pond, which supplied pike, perch, and trout. Eventually, Katherine von Bora made arrangements to purchase a farm at Zulsdorf, two days distant from Wittenberg. She loved the place, so that Luther often joked with her about it, calling her Lord Katie or the Lady of Zulsdorf. The farm provided poultry and pork. Later on, Katherine von Bora wanted to purchase a place closer to Wittenberg. Though she eventually succeeded, it didn't work out as planned. In addition to all of the gardening and farming, Lord Katie looked after matters of drink. Taking over the brewing license that had been held by the monks, she made beer herself. In fact, she was able to convince the city to ban the dumping of garbage into the Elbe River on Tuesdays of every week—the day on which she drew water for brewing. And she also provided wine for the household. In his later years, Luther called her the brewmistress, bragging of the quality of both her beer and her wine.

Amidst all of the hubbub and confusion in the Luther household, Katherine von Bora bore six children. The firstborn was Hans, named for his grandfather. Then Luther got to know firsthand about the diapers he had written about earlier. As Hans grew, his father spoke of his filling the house with his crying and also of his relieving himself in every corner. When the diapers ran out, little Hans apparently ran bare-bottomed, as children in other ages traditionally did. Hans was followed by Elizabeth; Magdalena, named for Mumme Lena; Martin; Paul, named for the Apostle; and finally Margarethe, named after her grandmother.

Two of the girls died young, giving the Luthers firsthand experience with one of the deepest tribulations of parenthood. Elizabeth did not survive her first year. Magdalena was fourteen at the time of her death in 1542. Her loss pitched Martin and Katie into profound grief. Luther wondered how the world could look so dark even while Magdalena had gone to the resurrection.

With her husband's foibles and all of the household duties, Katherine von Bora hardly had time to participate in the theological discussions that regularly developed around the table. Students, guests, faculty friends, and neighbors like Philip Melanchthon, who lived around the corner, addressed questions and raised issues. Luther, frequently a little talkative with Katie's beer, took them up in extended conversations. The students took notes, eventually publishing them in Luther's *Table Talk*—a valuable, informal source of insight into Luther's thinking, even if not always completely reliable. When Katherine did enter the conversation, she showed herself well aware of what was going on. Luther encouraged her, especially in her studies of Scripture. At one point, Luther offered her a cash prize if she read the Bible through. Katherine also encouraged Luther's theological writing: she was the one who pushed him to write a reply to Erasmus.

Evenings in the old cloister were often musical. In addition to everything else, Luther was an accomplished musician. He had a fine tenor voice, with such a range that some even describe him as an alto. He also played the lute, a difficult twelve-stringed medieval instrument the size of a guitar, and was knowledgeable enough to write harmony and to compose a number of hymns. Neighbors and students often came by in the evenings to play and sing.

It must have been quite a household. Where cloistered monks had once walked in silent pairs, children now ran and shouted, students argued and kept a running written tab of Luther's irreverences, and visitors came and went seemingly by the dozens. Everything was hustle and bustle.

As the years went by, the Luthers' love for one another deepened. He teased her tenderly, punning on her name—the German word for *chains* sounds much like Katie—and clearly cherished her. While she also referred to him by his title, as Doctor Luther, and continued to use the formally polite German address with him, she clearly shared his deep affection. A letter written shortly before Luther's death shows the relationship in characteristic form. Frequently required by his work to be away from home, Luther regularly wrote to Katherine and the children. On February 10, 1546, he wrote:

> To the saintly worrying Lord Katherine Luther, doctor at Zulsdorf and Wittenberg, my gracious dear wife:
>   We thank you heartily for being so worried that you can't sleep, for since you started worrying about us, a fire broke out near my door

and yesterday, no doubt due to your worry, a big stone, save for the dear angels, would have fallen and crushed us like a mouse in a trap. If you don't stop worrying, I'm afraid the earth will swallow us. Haven't you learned the Catechism and don't you believe? Pray and let God worry. "Cast your burden on the Lord." We are well except that Jonas banged his ankle. He is jealous of me and wanted to have something the matter with him, too. We hope soon to be released from this assignment and come home.

With her real-estate dealings, scrimping, and saving, Katherine von Bora had not only managed the household but managed to build up quite a nest egg. At Luther's death, his estate was valued at more than a half-million dollars in today's currency. Given Luther's habits with money, there is no doubt that the estate is Katherine von Bora's achievement. But it didn't last long. Shortly after Luther's death, Charles V finally made good on the Edict of Worms, sending his Spanish troops across the farm at Zulsdorf into Wittenberg itself to put an end to the Lutheran Reformation. Katherine von Bora lost everything. She died not long after, in 1551. Her last words, spoken to her sons, were, "I will stick to Christ like a burr to a topcoat."

Katherine von Bora's contribution to the Reformation has far outlasted her real-estate acumen. She and Luther shared their family vocation, leaving a lasting witness to the power of the Gospel even in the tumult of the household.

But that is getting far ahead of the rest of the story. In the later 1520s, somewhere around 1527, there was an important change in the Reformation. While the cries of little Hans echoed through the house, Katherine von Bora was learning the true proportions of what she had married into. Luther, still vulnerable to his own struggles with himself, was still marveling at the delight of finding pigtails on his pillow. Out of the disorder and chaos of all of the conflicts, theological and social, of the early 1520s, some order was beginning to emerge. The question was what form it would take.

CHAPTER 7

RENEWAL AND REFORM: 1527–1532

E ver since Luther had returned from the Wartburg, things had been a mess. There was controversy on all sides—with traditional Roman Catholics, the Radical Reformers, Erasmus, the southwest Germans, and the Swiss. With the Peasants' War, the mess turned to chaos. In all of this, there were two sources of stability. Luther could still count on the support of the elector of Saxony, even when Frederick the Wise died and was replaced by his brother, John the Constant. And Katherine von Bora had also brought some order, even after young Hans started to test his early mobility around the house.

The question between about 1527 and 1532 was how to put things together again. One level concerned Wittenberg and electoral Saxony. To this point, the Reformation there had been limited to the faculty and some pastors, with the support of the politicians. All of them, led by Luther, were concerned to consolidate their witness to the Gospel and to apply it in the lives of the congregations.

At another level, the question of order involved the empire and the rest of Europe. The church, to this point united in spite of all of the difficulties, appeared to be flying apart. Somehow, it had to come together, lest the divisions become permanent. The efforts toward unity, locally and internationally, frame Luther's story in the late 1520s and early 1530s. In the process, he wrote some of his most important work.

MORE TROUBLE WITHIN

Before taking on such externals, however, Luther had to deal with himself—both physically and spiritually. Considering all he had been through over the years, his health had held up remarkably well. But in 1526, Luther's health broke—at least temporarily. He had his first bout with kidney stones, a problem that became particularly acute in the later 1530s and bothered him regularly thereafter. Besides the torturous pain that generally accompanies "stone," as he called it, there can be other problems with kidneys—jaundice, uremic poisoning, and the like. There is some suggestion that Luther may also have had a minor heart attack during this time—the malady or condition that eventually killed him.

But for all of this, Luther's more serious problem was spiritual. Since returning from the Wartburg, he continued to have occasional struggles with the deep dread, or *Anfechtung*, that had plagued him for more than ten years. But early in 1527, the attacks intensified and were prolonged. In fact, it has been called Luther's lost year. Early on, friends, unable to rouse him in his office, peered through the keyhole to see him unconscious on the floor. They removed the door, brought him to, and when he described the trouble he had been having, stayed and sang with him. It was medicine to him; he asked that they return regularly for more songs. But the dread proved stronger than the music. At another point, he was laid low for a week, desperately trying to fight off the fears and doubts assailing him. "Christ holds me but by a thin thread," he wrote to a friend. At times he seemed convinced that the thread had broken or was breaking. It was the end of 1527 before his letters omitted reference to his spiritual battles.

One factor may have been his physical troubles. His ailments brought home the reality of death's power once more. Another factor may have been the death of his and Katherine's daughter Elizabeth. She was a fragile child who didn't survive infancy. But his own giftedness and the controversies in which it enveloped him may periodically have overwhelmed him.

Luther had his own way of interpreting his struggles with dread. "Faith has a magnet's head," he once wrote to another person having similar difficulties. "It draws its opposite, namely, unbelief." He saw his personal battles as part of the unfolding conflict between Christ and Satan, convinced that the devil, "who has a nose for faith," had smelled his confidence in the Lord Jesus and had come to undo it. He fought back with the word of God and prayer, convinced that they were his only recourse against such power. He also knew some more immediate sources of help. "Flee solitude and seek the company of another," he wrote to someone who besought him for help. So, too, he urged people in similar circumstances to play games, to joke and sing.

Luther's own extended firsthand experience with *Anfechtung*, along with his practical approaches to it with others, gave him a wide reputation as a pastor. He dealt with people directly and also kept up a wide correspondence. Luther's letters of spiritual counsel remain one of the very best introductions to his work.

Luther was also famous for his prayers. They were direct, forthright, almost impertinent or cheeky. For some reason, he liked to pray in front of an open window. He would remind God of the Second Commandment, the command to pray, then name the difficulty and insist on God's help. It was one such prayer that revived the friendship between Luther and Melanchthon in 1527. Melanchthon and his wife had lost a child. Melanchthon was having his own struggles with despair and was in bed when Luther came to visit. Luther listened to his younger colleague, threw open the window, and prayed with such ardor and tenderness that Melanchthon's old antipathies melted away.

In his struggles, Luther also knew the value of hard work, drawing him out of himself and focusing his attention on other matters. So through the later 1520s, he continued to rework his translation of the Bible. He gave lectures on some of the later letters of Paul and studied John's Gospel intently.

Continued troubles with the Turks and the threat of the Edict of Worms, along with recent memories of the Peasants' War, raised military questions for Luther that he had to address. To complicate matters further, plague broke out in Wittenberg—the faculty withdrew to the city of Jena, where classes continued. Luther stayed behind, insisting on giving his lectures at the Black Cloister while also caring for plague victims. With all of this combined, he had more than enough to keep him occupied.

While he ran from his lecture rostrum to a plague bed, the Wittenberg Reformation was undergoing a transition that demanded his attention. His health returned, the dread subsided, and while juggling duties, he turned his attentions to the changing front of the reform, consolidating what had already been achieved and then taking the additional steps demanded.

LITURGICAL RENEWAL AND REFORM

Martin Luther was not a Lutheran. That term was a nasty nickname increasingly attached to him and his followers in the 1520s. It has stuck to the worldwide denomination that still bears his name. He was a Roman Catholic, born, baptized, and ordained as such. Even as an excommunicant and an outlaw, he continued to regard himself as a faithful member of the one, holy, catholic, and apostolic church. Again and again, especially over and against the powers of division, he spoke of the importance of staying within it—at least until much later in the Reformation. But Luther took steps that led in a different direction from his hopes and intentions for church unity.

The first and, in some ways, the most fateful step fell softly in 1525. Luther published a German revision of the Latin Mass to be used in Wittenberg and other parts of Saxony. The changes were minor but significant. Luther reoriented the liturgy, removing allusions to sacrifice to emphasize proclamation in both preaching and the sacraments. As he saw it, the real purpose of worship is not doing something for God—as though God needed anything—but to occasion God's caring for his people, handing over Christ's gifts and benefits in the preached word, baptism, and the Lord's Supper.

Some of the faithful around Wittenberg had questions about Luther's German Mass, preferring the familiar Latin one. They questioned, for example, all the hymn singing—a change Luther advocated strongly, writing some of the hymns himself. Many of them were not sure about receiving both the bread and the wine at the sacrament. Traditionally Catholics received the bread but not the wine. Recognizing this resistance, Luther was willing to make accommodations. As long as the Gospel is at work, he believed, liturgical forms can vary as they need to according to the circumstances.

Luther's freedom with the rubrics—commonly accepted liturgical rules—also encountered some hostilities far beyond Wittenberg. In late medieval and early modern European life, liturgy and politics were closely connected. Dating back almost a thousand years, the common form of worship—the Roman Mass—had been in use across the continent, east to west and, more importantly, south to north. Day in and day out, Sunday after Sunday, the Mass visibly expressed the unity of the church despite all the different forms of governance among the European peoples. In the minds of church authorities and political officials, including the emperor, the liturgy was to be everywhere and always, invariably the same. Reducing the rubrics to a local option and publishing the German Mass had implications far beyond what Luther was contemplating. It amounted to a declaration of independence by the Saxon church. So when Charles V did get his chances to deal directly with the Wittenberg reform, in 1530 and again in 1548, he brushed right past the theological issues, demanding an account of the liturgical variations. As far as he was concerned, that was the issue.

In 1527, Luther recognized that further steps would have to be taken, steps that would further solidify the reform. To this point, his efforts had been an important part of what has in recent years been called "a reform movement within the church catholic." The leaders had been a loosely affiliated group of friends, colleagues, and allies gathered around Luther. Some, like Melanchthon and Justus Jonas, were on the faculty. Others, like John Bugenhagen and Nicholas von Amsdorf, were pastors. Still others, such as George Spalatin, had the political connections to gain support. Academic friendships, along with Luther's writings, had spread the movement to some other parts of Germany, the city of Nuremburg for example, and some surrounding territories. Frederick the Wise and then John the Constant had sheltered the movement as it had grown. But still it was without any formal organization, held together loosely by a common witness to the Gospel, a shared if sometimes critical loyalty to Luther, and the general conviction that there was no need to break off from the Catholic church and try to establish another.

But in 1526 and 1527, a conviction was growing that something more was needed. Still local, and still provisional, some means was needed to care for church life until the issues raised by the Reformation were settled—something a little more organized and formal. It was called the Saxon Church Visitation. Teams of parish visitors, usually consisting of a pair of theologians along with a pair of canon lawyers, were deputized to assess the conditions in particular congregations and to make recommendations for reform. The lawyers went along because the parishes were part of the governmental structure. Luther was in on some of the original visits, as was Melanchthon.

The parish visitors got an earful. Germans' delight in beer is legendary, and public drunkenness was a common problem. Wittenberg was notorious for its prostitutes, who ensnared Luther's students along with the general population. There was no shortage of other opportunities for adultery and fornication. Movement from farm to city, as today in developing economies around the world, has a way of destabilizing family life. And with a modern capitalist system in its early stages, there were lots of financial troubles. Usury or loan-sharking was a particular problem in Luther's mind, even if the interest rates were comparatively low by contemporary standards. He preached against greed as much as any other sin.

The pastors were not guiltless, especially in sexual matters. The most common way around the old celibacy requirements had been the employment of a cook who became a de facto wife. In some parts of the church the bishops even charged a tax on such arrangements. In one area, the visitors found virtually 90 percent of the preachers living in illicit arrangements. But the sexual violation was just one level of the problem. Women who got involved in such relationships lacked the legal protection of marriage, and their children were stigmatized as "priest's bastards."

If Luther was prepared for the visitors' reports, reading them with a seasoned and practical eye, Melanchthon was horrified. His orientation in Erasmus's humanism had left him prone to moral outrage; he also remembered the common criticism, that Luther's emphasis on freedom would lead to moral laxity. Now, even if it couldn't be attributed to his older colleague's preaching, here was degeneracy staring him right in the face.

"The world is like a drunken peasant trying to mount a horse," Luther once said. "If he gets up one side, he falls off the other." As the Wittenbergers sifted through the visitors' findings, they had to lean to the other side of the horse. As they did, their Reformation changed. To this point, the issue had been freeing the conscience from the burden of the law. But now the issue was how to proclaim the Gospel while taking up a traditional assignment of the church, the moral order of the community. For prophets, pulling people together into a movement is sufficient. Dealing with public life demands some structure.

As the Reformation shifted fronts, the Reformers broke into conflict. Melanchthon made the first proposal for taking on the new concern. If the problem is public morals, the solution is the law—hard and heavy. Melanchthon set to work on a document entitled *The Instructions for Parish Visitors*. It went through several preliminary versions; Luther and others also had a hand in it. But the alarmed voice sounding in it was clearly that of Master Philip, urging preachers to set out the threats of the law, both in this life and the life to come.

The call for the law brought a response, as would be expected. It came from Johann Agricola, the third leader with Luther and Melanchthon from the early years of the Reformation. He argued that trying to make people legally righteous by scaring the hell out of them doesn't produce faith but self-protection. The solution to the moral problem rests in setting out the Gospel "in all its sweetness," as he said, so that people will be moved by Christ's self-sacrifice to rethink their own behavior.

It took a while for the conflict to break into the open. When it did, it lasted from the spring of 1528 into the fall. It escalated to the point where the faculty at the University of Vienna offered Melanchthon a position so that he could get out of Wittenberg. For one reason or another, perhaps because he knew both Melanchthon and Agricola well enough to see where they were misunderstanding one another, Luther didn't take the controversy very seriously. But by fall, the elector was getting concerned and asked Luther to settle it. The three theologians met at the elector's residence in the town of Torgau, and Luther worked out a settlement.

Though commonly underestimated and overlooked, Luther's resolution of this controversy was crucially important to him and what was now becoming the Lutheran Reformation. It showed the way for taking on the problem of public morals.

For much of his monastic life, Luther had been thinking through what the Gospel does to the law. At one level, the implication couldn't be clearer: since Christ is the way, the truth, and the life, the law can no longer be decisive. Because Christ saves, Moses does not. In fact, as Luther said in a famous sermon of 1525, "How Christians Should Regard Moses," Moses, with his rules and laws, is dead. "His rule ended when Christ came." The Gospel is law-free, beyond any qualification or stipulation. When Christ takes hold in true faith, Moses' services are no longer needed.

But along the way, Luther had also recognized Moses' essential service. While legal requirements can neither save nor free, they provide order and safety, like the rules of a family. Though the rules can't produce it, they can point to the righteousness of faith—the joyous service of God, the neighbor, and the earth that happens as the heart is held in Christ's tender grasp. So just as Moses loses his power when Christ takes over, when faith recedes, Moses returns. In the end, when Christ has defeated the powers of death and desolation, the law will be no more. In the meantime, the powers of sin, death, and devil being at work in this life, Moses still has work to do.

Both Melanchthon and Agricola had each fallen off their own side of the horse, going to one end of the dialectic while losing the other. Melanchthon expected Moses to perform some of Christ's work; Agricola wanted Christ to do some of Moses' work. Settling the controversy between them, Luther proposed another distinction, this one between public and personal faith. Public faith involves the general conviction that God rewards good behavior and punishes bad. Rules and regulations provide for at least provisional forms of peace and justice in the rough and tumble of sinful life. Personal faith, the conviction that

Jesus died for my sins and will raise me from the dead, is the work of the Spirit of the risen Christ accomplished through the Gospel.

This gives the church a double responsibility. First, last, and always, its calling is the proclamation of the Gospel in its preached and sacramental forms. For the time being, as long as sin and death remain, however, it also has to lend a voice to Moses, clearly setting out the demands and requirements of the law.

Initially Melanchthon and Agricola were apparently satisfied with Luther's resolution. The controversy ended. But the issue surfaced later, becoming a troublesome point in the Lutheran reform and, in the mind of its critics, for later Lutheranism.

THE CATECHISMS

Whatever else could have been said about Luther the reformer, he was always a preacher. All the way through the reform, he had been explaining the practical consequences of his biblical and theological studies for the laity. He had preached the Ten Commandments, the Apostles' Creed, and the Lord's Prayer. Besides preaching, he had published pamphlets on the sacraments.

The new situation in Wittenberg and electoral Saxony demanded longer-term measures. For some time, Luther had been considering writing a catechism, a small handbook defining the basics of the faith. There were many such documents in circulation, some of them dating back to the early years of the church, others more contemporary. Often medieval catechisms included the Lord's Prayer, the Ave Maria, and other devotions. Luther suggested to several of his friends, among them Melanchthon and Agricola, that they should try their hand at a catechism. Agricola produced one; Melanchthon's efforts have been lost.

Finally, in 1528, Luther decided that he should see to the matter himself. In fact he wrote two, the *Small Catechism* for parents to use in instruction of their children, and the *Large Catechism* for use by preachers and teachers. Written in Luther's direct, down-to-earth German, the *Small Catechism* was originally printed up on the equivalent of posters that could be hung in the family kitchen. The *Large Catechism* gets its name from the fact that it is longer and more explanatory. There Luther is sometimes somewhat critical of alternative views but generally just as direct and plain-spoken as in the *Small*.

The two catechisms share a common structure, reflecting the settlement Luther struck between Melanchthon and Agricola. The Ten

Commandments come first, followed by the Apostles' Creed, and the Lord's Prayer. They make up what might be called "the word" section of Luther's catechisms, summarizing what the law requires, what God does, and how we can pray. Then follows treatment of the sacraments, baptism and the Lord's Supper. Later, Luther added an explanation of the keys and confession, that is, Christ's authorization for declaration of the words of forgiveness, and a form of personal confession. He also added a table of duties, describing the vocations of everyday life.

Although he is often criticized for emphasizing them, the Ten Commandments are first in Luther's catechism because the requirements of the law are first in human experience. We are born under the law, in a context of life where demands and obligations—in relation to God, the neighbor, and the earth—are the inescapable reality. The Ten Commandments, in that sense, are not Christian or even religious teachings: they summarize what life requires of everyone. Creatures, beings who do not have life in themselves but receive it through others, have to get along with their Creator, with the other creatures who shape and condition life, and with creation itself. The creed declares how Christ has entered this context of requirement, taking the obligations upon himself to break people loose from the powers of desolation. It further declares the work of the Holy Spirit, who, convicting people of their sins, at the same time creates the faith God requires. Then the Lord's Prayer properly follows, teaching us, in Luther's words, "how to seek and obtain the help that we need."

Both baptism and the Lord's Supper had drawn fire, baptism from the Radical Reformers, especially the Anabaptists, and the Lord's Supper in the debate over the real presence of Christ at the table. Luther added the explanations of the sacraments, with the keys and confession, to set them out clearly, plainly, in their down-to-earth character.

The *Small Catechism,* in chart and pamphlet form, quickly became one of the most important documents of the Lutheran Reformation. It moved the village altar into the family kitchen, literally bringing instruction in the faith home to the intimacies of family life. It has gone with Lutherans around the world in both immigration and mission, remaining the best-known and most dearly beloved Lutheran statement of faith. The *Large Catechism* has never been as widely used. Still it is one of the best introductions to Luther's understanding of the Christian faith. In fact, he considered the two catechisms, with *The Bondage of the Will,* his very best work.

THE MAKINGS OF AN INTERLUDE

Through the early 1520s, the Emperor Charles V was so mired in other problems that he couldn't make good on the threat he had levied in the Diet of Worms of 1521, where he had banned Luther and his followers. His biggest problem at the time was the Turks, though the papacy was hardly cooperative.

The Ottoman Turks were led by one of the great strategists in military history, Sulieman the Magnificent. For centuries, the Turks had been pushing their way up into the Balkans. Under Sulieman, they had mobilized even more effectively, extending their lines all the way to Vienna, effectively the back door to Western Europe—the doorstep of Charles V's Hapsburg holdings in nearby Hungary, ruled by his brother Ferdinand. Sulieman's land attacks were joined at sea by a Turkish pirate, Barbarossa. While he couldn't match the 1527 siege Sulieman laid on Vienna, Barbarossa mixed it up in the Mediterranean shipping lanes, causing particular problems for Italian maritime centers, like Venice, dependent on the sea.

There was another dimension to the Turkish threat besides the military. Through the papacy, Western Europe had laid claim to Christ's assertion in Matthew 28:19, "All authority in heaven and earth had been given to me." Regarding themselves as Christ's earthly vicar, medieval popes since the thirteenth century had claimed in their office to embody his lordship over all the earth. The Turks were "the infidel," part of a larger Muslim community of faith that had been challenging Christendom's claims in the southern corners of Europe, in Spain as well as the Balkans, for hundreds of years. In the thirteenth century, the Europeans had mobilized four great crusades as well as some smaller ones against Islam—aggression well remembered even today among Muslims. Sulieman's successes not only threatened lands and peoples but also undermined the European claim to religious preeminence. Luther was as aware of this as any other European, praying regularly against the Turks.

For Charles V, however, the immediate problem was troops. He needed a sufficient supply from his subjects to counter Sulieman's strategic brilliance. To reach this end, he had to compromise, backing off on the Edict of Worms for the time being. That gave the forces behind Luther and other parties in the Reformation time to consolidate their reforms without the threat of violence.

Clement VII took over the papacy in 1522, holding the office until 1534. He followed Pope Leo's strategy for dealing with the

Reformation, attempting to stifle and repress it at all costs. Clement was willing to compromise with Charles V because he needed Charles's military power to enforce the Edict of Worms. But he also considered Charles his one real rival in Europe, and he wouldn't pass by an opportunity to undermine him. So while Charles V was marshaling his forces against the Turks, in 1526 his troops and Clement's broke into open conflict. This resulted in one of the delightful ironies of the Reformation: while protecting the papacy against the perceived Lutheran threat, Charles was holding Clement in prison. Despite his own antipathies to reform, Clement wound up diverting Charles and allowing further room for the Lutheran movement.

CHAPTER 8

AUGSBURG AND BEYOND

P hilip Melanchthon was walking back to Wittenberg after a visit to his home in the south of Germany, Wurtemberg, when he encountered Philip of Hesse. The latter was an enthusiastic supporter of the Reformation. As Landgrave of Hesse, leader of a state around Frankfurt, he was extraordinarily well placed by both power and location to help in dealings between the east-central German Lutherans and the southwest German and Swiss Reformers.

Despite the interlude of relative calm, Philip of Hesse recognized the dangers. Not only had the papacy implacably opposed the Reformation, but Charles V had already at Worms announced his intention to bring the Reformation to a forcible end. No matter what their differences in views of the Sacrament of the Altar, the Lutherans and the Upper Rhine Germans and Swiss should have at least agreed to disagree on the matter and made common cause against the emperor, as well as the papacy. But for both sides, other considerations prevailed. Despite the good efforts of Philip of Hesse, Philip Melanchthon, Martin Bucer, and others, no lasting compromise was ever struck. The Lutherans and the Reformed, as they have been commonly called, or Lutheranism and Protestantism, remained divided.

No doubt, Luther's personality was one of the reasons. Events had conspired to make him a symbol of the Reformation, elevating him to a prophetic standing. Fighting his way through one controversy after another, he had accepted this symbolic authority as a vocation. As tender, humorous, and soft-handed as he could be in matters of faith, in controversy he could also be harsh, arbitrary, and doctrinaire. Though he could compromise when trust was justified, trust didn't come easily to him, especially when there was evidence of deceit or betrayal. So he stuck with Philip Melanchthon, even when he knew they had serious theological differences. He could even later yield for a time to Martin Bucer, whom he seriously distrusted. But generally, when his suspicions were aroused, they froze in place.

The southwest Germans and Swiss repeatedly made Luther the issue. But to Luther himself, there were other considerations beyond his person. One was the nature of the sacrament itself. As we have seen, with Ulrich Zwingli, Oecolampadius, and their successors in southwest Germany, Luther rejected the doctrine of transubstantiation. It was a needless abstraction, a philosophical explanation of Christ's presence that substituted itself for faith in the promise. Christ's words, "This is my body given for you," "This cup is the New Testament in my blood, shed for you and for many," were for Luther the very center of the sacrament. The sacrament is a testament, a point where the risen Christ is actually and really present to distribute to the faithful the benefits of his death and resurrection: "the forgiveness of sins, life, and salvation." Everything depends on this, that Christ in the speaking of the word joins himself to the bread and wine to literally hand over the goods here and now to those who eat and drink. To compromise at this point, Luther thought, is to compromise the Gospel itself.

Life demands concessions. But the swirling events of the 1520s, the chaos of the Peasants' War, and even the moral disorder found in the visitations had deepened Luther's conviction that the end of time was breaking in, that the present was decisive, and that Christ could return at any moment. That conviction would grow even more profound in the later 1530s and 1540s. So, when pressured to yield, Luther couldn't give, and neither could those gathered with him.

Faced with Luther's intransigence and the support he maintained in Wittenberg, Philip of Hesse decided that the only way to an alliance between the Lutherans and the Reformed was to bring Luther and Zwingli together face-to-face. When he procured their agreement, they sat down together in one of the most famous meetings of the Reformation, across the table from one another in the city of Marburg.

When Luther and Zwingli met at the Marburg Colloquy in October 1529, words became the issue. According to legend, Luther drew back the tablecloth and wrote the phrase *Hoc est corpus meum*, "This is my body," on the table. Apparently he wrote it in chalk, underlining the *est* or *is* several times. Zwingli was just as unyielding, insisting that the word *is* means "represents" or "signifies." Both Luther and Zwingli were equally convinced of their points. Luther insisted that Christ is present to bestow his gifts and the faith that receives them.

Zwingli maintained that Christ has ascended into heaven, and it is therefore up to faith to discern what the elements represent. With that, Philip of Hesse's efforts foundered.

In fact, the meeting was friendlier than might have been expected. Luther was asked to write a summary of the discussion, an assignment that he carried out in what has been called the *Marburg Colloquy*. Both the tone and the content indicate that the conversations had been productive, in spite of suspicions on both sides. Luther and Zwingli had agreed on fourteen out of fifteen points, everything except the sacrament itself.

With this, talk of an alliance ended—at least for a time. Efforts to resolve the issue would continue through the 1530s and into the 1540s, at one point very nearly succeeding. But for the immediate future, the Lutherans would have to go it alone.

ECUMENICAL POLITICS: THE EMPEROR'S EFFORTS

Though otherwise occupied with the Turks and the pope, Charles V still found time to deal with those supporting Luther and the Wittenberg reform, at least occasionally.

The first overture had developed at the Diet of Speyer in 1526. In urgent need of support against the incursions of the Turks near the Hapsburg holdings in Austria-Hungary, Charles V called a diet to consider the religious problem posed by the Reformers. Speyer, a beautiful town in the wine country of Germany southwest of Frankfurt, was set as the site for this assembly. But when the time came, Charles himself could not attend.

At the Diet of Speyer, John the Constant, carrying on Frederick the Wise's protection of the reform, had both direct support from his allies and some sympathy he could count on from the rest of the assembled German sovereigns. There was not enough support to rescind the Edict of Worms but enough to move around it. The diet did so by establishing the principle that the rulers could choose the religious affiliation of their own territory.

Though this principle had all the earmarks of a moderate compromise, the action at Speyer had both short- and long-term significance. In the short term, it meant that local rulers, like John and others who supported the Reformation, could legally carry it out in their own territories. As the Wittenbergers interpreted it, in fact, this was the legal basis for the Saxon Church Visitation. If Speyer's direction looked like the most reasonable step to take, however, its long-term significance was immediately apparent to Charles V, his brother Ferdinand, and all the others intent on preserving the religious unity of the empire and Europe. Allowing the rulers the freedom that the Saxons had already been employing was the beginning of the end of this unity.

The next time Charles V called a diet, also to meet in Speyer, this one in 1528, he was a little more circumspect. Unable to attend for the second time, he dispatched his brother Ferdinand to represent him. Ferdinand felt that he had the Reformation in his own backyard. For that reason, in addition to having a more fiery temperament, he was not about to make concessions to the Saxons or any others interested in reform. So when the second Diet of Speyer met, he announced that the compromise of the first diet of 1526 had been revoked, triggering a walkout by several territorial rulers in protest. It is from this incident that the name Protestant first arose, even though now it is used in a much wider sense.

As much as he opposed the Reformation, Charles V still needed to be on good terms with those giving it political support. So, after Ferdinand pushed the Reformers, the emperor back-pedaled—or at least appeared to ease up some. The next time he called a diet, this one to meet in the southern city of Augsburg in May of 1530, he promised the Lutherans a chance to give an account of themselves—something the Saxons had been asking for ever since the first attempts to quash the indulgences controversy.

Originally, Frederick the Wise, George Spalatin, and Luther would have settled for a hearing. Now, with the widened disagreements, the Wittenberg Reformers wanted a council of the church—a meeting of all of the bishops of the church—to consider the theological issues that had been raised. Seven ancient ecumenical councils were recognized by the church; three or four more, with varying degrees of success, had met in the fifteenth century. Luther had formally appealed for such a council in 1518. But in the later 1520s, the Lutherans didn't just appeal. They made some demands: that the council include all the bishops, that it be free from papal interference, that it meet on German soil, and that it recognize no other authority than the Bible.

Seeing a council as a threat to their own claims to be Christ's earthly vicars, embodying his rule on earth, neither Leo nor Clement was about to accede to such demands, even if Charles himself were to insist. Recognizing these political realities, however reluctantly, the available half-loaf really did look better. If there would be no council in the near future, Charles's announcement of the diet at Augsburg appeared at least to present an opening. He specifically wanted an account of the liturgical changes implemented in electoral Saxony. Along with that, perhaps the Lutherans could also air the theological matters that had driven them and their reform.

With this hope propelling them, the Elector John put his theologians to work. They had some resources to work with, especially the *Marburg Colloquy*, and they could produce more. Though the route was longer and more winding than it first appeared, the result was a defining document of the Lutheran reform and later Lutheranism.

THE AUGSBURG CONFESSION

Preparing for the Diet of Augsburg, the Lutheran theologians wrote one document and compiled the basis of a second. Then after Melanchthon and the politicians arrived at Augsburg, having left Luther behind for safekeeping at a castle in the town of Coburg, they discovered that the promised openness was quickly evaporating. With this, Master Philip set to work editing and rewriting the preliminary work. The resulting document is known among Lutherans as the *Augsburg Confession*, from the Latin name of the city.

The Lutheran theologians had followed a basic assumption, one that shows how at odds they were with both Roman Catholic authorities and the southwest German and Swiss Reformers. For the papacy, the church was a hierarchy of power extending from Jesus Christ through the papacy to the bishops, who in turn authorized the priests to administer the sacraments. For Charles V and the politicians, what made the church was the liturgy, the common practice of the sacraments, and universal rules and regulations for the activities of the clergy. For the southwest Germans and the Swiss, more influenced by humanism, the marks of the church were the faith and obedience of the people.

For more than a decade, Luther and his colleagues had been protesting both the hierarchical and the sacramental character of Roman Catholicism. More recently, they had also rejected Zwingli's understanding of the Lord's Supper and the notion of the church that goes with it. Luther had written a *Confession concerning Christ's Supper*, arguing just these points. The word *confession* is more significant than it looks. For as Luther and his company saw it, what makes the church is neither its officers nor its people, but the word of God preached and embodied in the sacraments. The church comes into being when it *confesses*—when it speaks the word by which God creates, redeems, and produces faith in those who hear it. With this in mind, the logic was simple. If Charles would give them a hearing and if the southwest Germans and the Swiss couldn't agree on a common theology, then, the Lutherans would *confess*—that is, they would set out the theological convictions and assumptions that guided them in their preaching and teaching. Along the way, they would honor Charles's request to explain their liturgical revisions.

The first document they produced in preparation for the diet was drafted at a meeting in the town of Schwabach. These *Schwabach Articles* were apparently a group effort. Melanchthon had a significant part in their writing; sometimes Luther's touch also shows itself. Some of the other Wittenbergers were also involved. Compared to the *Marburg Colloquy,* which Luther had written at Philip of Hesse's request, and the later *Augsburg Confession,* the Schwabach statement is not as strong. But the theologians were satisfied with it, and Melanchthon brought it along.

In another meeting in Torgau, the Wittenbergers started work on Charles's request for a specific explanation of their liturgical changes. From the evidence, it appears that this document wasn't completed.

With this material at hand, a group of theologians and politicians left Wittenberg in late April or early May of 1530, journeying southwesterly through electoral Saxony toward Augsburg. They left Luther at the Coburg, sixty miles from Augsburg, because it was as close as he could get to the diet while remaining under the elector's protection. Gregorius Bruck, who served as chancellor under the electors and Melanchthon, would take the lead when they arrived in Augsburg.

Residing in Coburg was difficult for Luther. For a man accustomed to hard work and full days, enforced inactivity can be a real crucifixion. Luther missed Katie and his growing family. He wrote a wonderful letter to young Hans, fantasizing a garden playground. He also received word from home of his father's death, which grieved him. For his father Luther wrote a beautiful commentary on one of his favorite Psalms, 118. He also worried about Melanchthon, whose inclination to compromise had become well known. Messengers went back and forth between Augsburg and Coburg, but Luther complained of being tortured to death by silence.

In the meantime, Chancellor Bruck and Melanchthon had their hands full. When they arrived, they found in circulation a pamphlet assembled by Johann Eck, longtime opponent of Luther and the reform.

Culling through Luther's and Melanchthon's writings and throwing in some choice selections from the Radical Reformers, Eck had published his *404 Articles* to make his enemies look as seditious and hostile as possible. If the Lutherans were going to be given an opportunity to define themselves, Eck would do his part to make them look like the threat to the empire they had always represented to him.

Recognizing the potential damage, aware now that what had looked like an opening was closing fast, Melanchthon set to work on the preliminary resources he carried with him. Consulting the *Marburg Colloquy*, he edited the *Schwabach Articles*, using them as a basis for the first eighteen articles of what became the *Augsburg Confession*. He then added three articles of his own on issues he thought to be of particular concern, such as the freedom of the will, the causes of sin, and the relationship of faith and good works. He finished the work on liturgical matters begun at Torgau, identifying them together in seven articles on abuses that had been corrected by their reforms. Consulting with Bruck and others, relaying messages from Luther, Melanchthon revised right up to the time when the twenty-eight articles of the *Augsburg Confession* were to be presented.

The presentation was nearly canceled. Diets being the kind of assemblies that they were, the town was packed and abuzz with expectation. Augsburg townspeople, like city dwellers in many other parts of Germany, were generally sympathetic to Luther and the reform. The authorities feared a possible riot. The elector was understandably nervous, while those fighting to preserve the status quo were looking for ways to tip things back in their own direction.

Finally, word arrived in Augsburg that the emperor and his retinue had been sighted, winding their way up the River Lech toward the city. The elector sent his representative, hoping to get a word in before the proceedings got started. Others also went out to meet Charles V, to accompany him into the city. When the parties met outside the city, the papal *nuncios*—the pope's official representatives—raised the pope's colors. Charles dismounted, getting on his knee to indicate his loyalty. The others in the party did likewise. Only the Lutherans remained standing. This offended Charles to the point where he considered suspending the discussion altogether. In Augsburg itself, a Corpus Christi procession took place, the reserved bread of the sacrament being carried in a monstrance, a sacred container, on a pole at the head of the parade. Again, the Lutherans refused to kneel. Once more, it looked like things would finish before they even started.

Still, the schedule unfolded as planned. When the time came for the presentation, on June 25, the diet adjourned to a smaller episcopal palace—a bishop's residence—the assumption being that a removed location would keep down the crowd, forestalling the possibility of a riot. The Lutherans countered with a move of their own. It was hot enough that the windows would have to be opened. A reader was selected who had enough voice to be heard by those gathered around the building. He read the confession aloud for all to hear. Maybe it was the heat, perhaps the length—Charles V fell sound asleep.

Others were much more impressed. Melanchthon had achieved his goal. Stepping around the attempts to portray them as malicious, he had presented the Lutheran confession in a positive light, demonstrating its anchorage in the larger Catholic tradition of the church. In fact, the bishop of Augsburg—no friend of the Reformation—is said to have remarked, "This is nothing but the Catholic truth." Luther also expressed his approval, writing that he liked Philip's confession right well, even though he was not capable himself of such pussyfooting.

Signed by Elector John, Philip of Hesse, and three other regional sovereigns, as well as by representatives of two imperial cities, the *Augsburg Confession* came very close to bringing about a settlement—as close as anything achieved between 1517 and 1555. When he woke up to what the Lutherans had done, Charles set up negotiations. At the diet itself, Eck drafted a rejoinder to the *Augsburg Confession*. When Charles rejected the first draft as too "long winded and vicious" to be helpful, Eck and other traditional Roman Catholic theologians prepared another. It, too, was read, though Charles apparently still was not satisfied. The Lutherans were refused a copy of this document, called *The Confutation*. After the diet, Charles appointed a Committee of Fourteen, which met through June into August. They reached agreement on twenty-seven of the twenty-eight articles, the negotiations finally breaking down on Article 21 concerning the invocation of the saints. When he suspended negotiations, Charles V declared that the Lutheran confession had been repudiated, and he reinvoked the 1521 Edict of Worms, which had condemned the reform and outlawed those who followed it. He promised to use military force if the reforming territories did not consent to return to Catholic practices by April 15, 1531.

Though the negotiations failed, the *Augsburg Confession* survived. Reflecting the ecumenical orientation characteristic of the earlier years of the Reformation, diplomatically worded in plain language, it was recognized for its value by all parties. With Luther's *Small Catechism*, it has continued to be the common confession of Lutherans throughout the world.

AUGSBURG'S AFTERMATH

If the Lutherans didn't convince Charles V of their orthodoxy, they at least persuaded him of this: there would be no settlement of the conflict engendered by the Reformation without a council of the church. It wasn't much of a hope, of course. The emperor knew that as well as anyone. But maybe, just maybe, something could be done. In the meantime, there were a couple of important developments.

One was the Schmalkald League. If they couldn't form an alliance to the southwest, the group of seven that had signed the *Augsburg Confession* at least had firm agreement among themselves. So they met and agreed to mutual defense, should Charles actually attempt to enforce the Edict of Worms militarily. The League became the political-military arm of the Lutheran Reformation, expanding through the 1530s into the 1540s until at one point it was said to include about three-fourths of Germany. That was the only time that Germany could be called Lutheran, even though it wasn't yet a country and the alliance had become far more political than religious. Later in the sixteenth century, Roman Catholic forces would reclaim large portions of southern Germany. The Reformed, by that time Calvinists, would take the West and some portions of the North as well. The Lutherans would get pushed back into the East before the story ended, barely managing to hold that. While it lasted, however, at least into the early and mid- 1540s, the Schmalkald League showed the resolve and solidarity of many German states to stand fast at great risk with the Reformers and to oppose a return to Roman Catholic practices.

The other significant development came late in 1532, the so-called Nuremburg Standstill. Knowing that the pope was unlikely to convene a council, Charles V was also well aware of the force the Lutherans could muster, particularly through something like the Schmalkald League. The emperor wanted a time out that would hold things in place for the time being. So negotiations began at a diet in Regensburg in 1531 and were completed in the city of Nuremburg, which as one of the signing sovereignties to the *Augsburg Confession* had become and would long remain a center of Lutheranism. The Standstill was just that, an agreement to keep things in place until a council of the church could be assembled. It allowed the Lutherans to perpetuate the situation that had prevailed since the first Diet of Speyer.

Charles V's threats after the Diet at Augsburg did leave a serious theological issue standing, however. Romans 13 and 1 Peter 3 both enjoin Christians to obey the emperor. The Book of Revelation, with its more subversive visions of the beast, provides a biblical alternative. In the chaos of the

1520s, Luther had appealed to the epistles' injunctions, urging believers to practice what nowadays would be called passive resistance. Rather than resorting to arms, they were to absorb the consequences of political abuse, obey the law in temporal or secular matters, and trust in God.

In the early 1530s, the situation was becoming more complex. The emperor had reasserted his threat to bring the Reformation to an end by force and demanded the restoration of Roman Catholic liturgical practices. Although the Nuremburg Standstill neutralized the threat for the time being, the emperor's intentions were obvious to all. With this in mind, the Wittenberg theologians met to consider the question of resistance. Could the local sovereigns justifiably resist the emperor? Could violent resistance of a temporal authority be justified when religious conscience was at stake? While no record of the meeting survives, it was clear to all—Luther included—that the issue had to be rethought.

GOING HOME

Luther returned from the Coburg in good spirits, delighted to be back with his family. But it wasn't long before his health broke again, overwork being a clear factor. The kidney stones and heart problems that had troubled him in 1526 had let up some in the intervening years. In 1531 and 1532, new health problems arose, among them dizziness, fainting spells and a ringing—Luther described it as roaring or something like hearing distant church bells—that was particularly bothersome in the mornings. He was sometimes so exhausted that he couldn't work, taking days and weeks of what he jokingly called his vacation. He also had some serious headaches. The fainting spells were especially alarming. Several times, Katherine had to call on Justus Jonas and others for help, fearing that her husband was near death.

Ill health didn't impede the demands on Luther's work. John Bugenhagen, the city pastor whom Luther knew affectionately as Dr. Pommer, was closely involved in carrying the Lutheran reform to Denmark. He had gone there for some time in the late 1520s and left again for a couple of years in the early 1530s. In his absence, Luther took over his responsibilities. That meant preaching four times a week, in addition to preparing lectures for twice-a-week classes. Family responsibilities, along with the usual hubbub of the Black Cloister— part hospital, part hotel, part dormitory in addition to everything else—complicated matters still further. Luther was regularly consulted in matters of marriage law and the like, all the while supporting the continuing development of the Reformation. He also had the printers dogging him, wanting something more to put on the market. It was enough work for three or four people. Small wonder that he had trouble recovering good health.

THE JUSTIFYING WORD

In the early 1530s, political crises and poor health notwithstanding, the Wittenberg theologians made two important statements on what they regarded as the heart of the matter: justification by faith. One was by Melanchthon, begun in the oxcart that carried him away from the negotiations at Augsburg, rumbling its way back toward Wittenberg. The other, by Luther himself, developed characteristically in a commentary on a letter of Paul's, this one Galatians. It became one of Luther's greatest writings.

As proud as he was of the *Augsburg Confession*, Melanchthon was bitterly disappointed in the failure of the negotiations at Augsburg through the summer of 1530. He had held on for all he was worth, yielding as much as he conceivably could, to no avail. The *Confutation*, written by Johann Eck and few others, was no match for the *Augsburg Confession*, no matter what the emperor declared. It didn't have much standing then, and it has even less with Roman Catholics now. Denied a copy, Melanchthon still had the notes he and others had taken when it was read aloud at the diet. So, first in the oxcart and later back in Wittenberg, he went to work on refuting the *Confutation*, taking it apart theologically and developing the countervailing Lutheran argument.

The result, thoroughly edited and revised, is Melanchthon's *Apology of the Augsburg Confession*—not, as the name now suggests, an indication of repentance, but a formal, technical explanation of the faith set forth in the *Augsburg Confession*. The form gives contemporary readers difficulties. Melanchthon closely follows the conventions of medieval theological debate. But Article IV of the *Apology* repays the required effort. It is a fully developed statement of Melanchthon's understanding of the logic of justification by faith alone. Historians, knowing some of the difficulties that emerged in the later 1530s and early 1540s, cannot help but notice some subtle differences between Melanchthon and Luther. For example, Melanchthon works with a more positive appraisal of the law—hardly a surprise, given the earlier conflict with Agricola. But that just makes the *Apology* all the more interesting.

In July of 1532, Luther returned to Paul's Letter to the Galatians. He had lectured on it once before, in 1519, when he was first working through the implications of his exegetical breakthrough. Now he was a mature theologian, having worked with Paul's dialectic and his own for roughly a decade and a half. He had come to have a deep love for the epistle, calling it his biblical Katie von Bora. The lectures continued into December. Luther went over the notes some of his best students had taken, editing and revising. The *Galatians Commentary* was published in 1535 and became one of Luther's first major works to be translated into English.

In 1519, Luther's problem, like Paul's in the original setting of the Epistle to the Galatians, was a legalistic interpretation of the Gospel. By this interpretation, God's work in Christ Jesus is not sufficient in itself but requires completion by the obedience of the faithful to the law of Israel. In the early 1530s, with the change of fronts in the Reformation, Luther saw an additional problem: the old legalism still showed itself here and there, but it had been joined by license, disregard for the law altogether.

Responding to the new situation, Luther used Paul's argument to address both misunderstandings of the Gospel. On the one side, against legalism, Luther declared the justifying word. Taking hold of one's conscience, Christ bestows on a person an entirely new sense of standing in relation to God, the neighbor, and the earth. He frees a person from the law with all of its requirements so that the believer can enter joyously into everyday life. Every theological effort must be expended to keep the law from taking over the conscience with its claim to legitimize and control the defining relationships. At the same time, on the other front— against license—the law is shown to have its place. It is for the body; that is, it provides for the essential disciplines of life among sinners, asserting its grip when faith loses its hold.

In matters of faith, the highest art of the believer is to learn to ignore the law and all active attempts to achieve righteousness, confident that God will produce the good fruit desired. At the same time, in matters of everyday arrangements, the law still makes its claim, demanding attention.

Literally sick and tired, contended for and contending, Luther had gone once more to the word that he believed had driven the Reformation from the beginning all the way through—God's justification of the sinner. His Galatians commentary was quickly recognized for its depth and insight. Even now, nearly five centuries later, a great scholar of the Apostle Paul has argued that any serious study of Galatians has to begin with Luther's commentary. With *The Bondage of the Will* and his catechisms, it represents Luther's greatest work.

CHAPTER 9

CONFLICTS AND RECONCILIATIONS

L uther was not old when he returned in 1530 to Wittenberg from his stay in Coburg, at least by modern standards—just in his late forties. Some of them had been years of great adventure, especially the time leading up to the Diet of Worms in 1521. The decade of the 1520s had been more chaotic, with the initial energy and excitement of the reform threatening to dissipate and divide. Yet in the late 1520s, by improvisation more than plan, Lutheranism had begun to take on form, producing documents that still give it some of its basic character. Now, with all that excitement in the past, the 1530s and early 1540s continued as they had begun—in the slogging of the ordinary, two steps forward and then three back. It was progress, though an inch at a time, back home in Wittenberg, in discussions with the Reformed in southwest Germany and in Switzerland, and even in prospects for an ecumenical council.

REFINING AND REDEFINING THE REFORM

A Lutheran campus pastor who knew his history once offered an ironic observation on how reforms work: the first generation builds the fire; the second generation tends the fire; the third generation tries to keep the fire from going out; the fourth generation guards the place where it burned; the fifth generation tries to remember what started the fire and where it happened. Traditions have a way of degenerating, even—maybe especially—close to home.

Similarly, later generations of Lutherans saw the early Reformation as the recovery of "pure doctrine," the authoritative teachings of the church. Although they disagreed intensely among themselves, they shared the conviction that Luther's real achievement was to recover, preserve, and protect the pure teachings of the word of God. Perhaps for just this reason, they tended to minimize or overlook important differences among the Lutheran Reformers themselves. These differences, emerging in the 1530s and early 1540s, erupted after Luther's death. They are an important part of the story of the Reformation.

Both Luther and Melanchthon were convinced of the importance of pure or sound doctrine, but they had different ideas of its purpose. For Luther, always a preacher and a pastor as well as a professor, doctrine is important because of the way it shapes preaching. Even justification by faith alone, the most important teaching he discovered, is not an end in itself. It tells the preacher how Christ is to be passed on, with all his gifts and benefits: freely, without qualification, directly to the hearer. Melanchthon was a teacher, a humanist much more appreciative of the ancient Greek and Roman classics, eager for the practicalities of reforming the institutions of public life, such as the church and the schools, as well as personal morals. He has been remembered as the "teacher of Germany," his curriculum reforms shaping German university life for centuries. He wrote to his first biographer near the time of his death, "I have striven in everything I have done to contribute to the actual improvement of community life."

While there are some suggestions of differences between Luther and Melanchthon in the later 1520s and the early 1530s, Melanchthon's change of direction didn't show itself conspicuously until 1535. Other significant evidence of difference appeared after 1541. In hindsight, Melanchthon's program shows through. He shared deeply Luther's biblical conviction that the Gospel is God's unqualified word of pardon and release in Christ Jesus. But at the same time, he was rethinking some important aspects of Luther's theology, attempting to retool it in the direction of public and personal reform. Specifically, he was bothered by Luther's arguments on the bondage of the will and therefore the part that a person plays in conversion and in obeying the law.

Luther was aware of some of the developing differences. Sometimes Melanchthon even came to talk about some of the issues. At one point later on, Chancellor Bruck was dispatched by the elector who took over in the 1530s, John Frederick, to warn Luther that if he and Melanchthon got into a public conflict, the elector would have to close the university. The warning probably wasn't necessary. Luther generally interpreted the differences in friendship, minimizing them even when they involved some disappointment.

In 1535, however, the differences broke out in the open, if not between Luther and Melanchthon themselves, then among some other faculty and students. A friend of Melanchthon's proposed that human willing is a factor in conversion, alongside the word of God. The proposal was carefully qualified: if a person has to accept God's proffered grace, the acceptance is not a cause of conversion in itself but is something like a catalyst. But as Luther's own students and later Luther himself saw it, it was the old problem: If acceptance is necessary, a person has to be satisfied that such acceptance is significant. Then faith turns from the word to its own self, getting caught up in a vicious circle in which acceptance has to be accepted and then accepted again. Melanchthon eventually acknowledged that he was behind the proposal and withdrew it, recognizing the language as unclear.

Melanchthon made another revision in 1541 that caused problems, although it didn't lead to open conflict. Though he knew the work of others had contributed to the *Augsburg Confession* and its public character as a confession of the church, Melanchthon seems to have regarded it as personal property. In 1541, he published a new edition, changing the statement of Article X, concerning the Lord's Supper, in a way that he thought would be acceptable to the southwest Germans and the Swiss. French reformer John Calvin himself is said to have expressed approval. This time, it was old Dr. Eck who noticed the difference and publicized it, much to Luther's disappointment. For this reason, Lutherans ever since have given greater authority to the unaltered *Augsburg Confession.*

Another theological conflict broke out in Wittenberg in the later 1530s, but this time it wasn't Melanchthon but Johann Agricola who precipitated it. Returning to Wittenberg after several years' residence in Eisleben, where he taught Latin, Agricola gathered some followers who shared his conviction that not only Melanchthon but Luther himself had made too many concessions to the law. An anonymous set of theses circulated through the town, one of them the statement that the law belongs in the courthouse, not the church. Agricola was apparently still convinced that the "sweetness of the Gospel" works repentance, people being turned around by the conviction of Christ's goodness in sacrificing himself.

The controversy quickly turned ugly. Intimidated by Luther but still wanting to make his point, Agricola alternately conceded and tried to recover his ground. Luther became convinced that Agricola was playing deceitful games with him. He demanded that Agricola face him in a series of six disputations between 1536 and 1539, though toward the end Agricola didn't always show up. Although later historians commonly passed over the disputations on the basis of some of Luther's own comments about Agricola, they remain a classic statement of Luther's understanding of law and Gospel. "Insofar as Christ is raised in us, so far are we without the law, sin and death," he argued. "Insofar as Christ is not raised in us, so far are we under the law, sin and death." While schooling Agricola in the distinction, Luther clearly had Melanchthon in mind as well, particularly Melanchthon's attempt to use the law as a force in personal moral reform. Agricola eventually left Wittenberg to accept a position as court preacher in Berlin. Luther's distrust had been so aroused that he and Agricola never did come to agree.

Measuring the differences between Luther and Melanchthon is one of the most challenging and controversial aspects of Lutheran Reformation studies. At Luther's funeral, Melanchthon acknowledged his difficulties with Luther's teachings on the bound will, doing so in some pointed terms. But apparently, as much as Luther insisted that faith has to take priority over love in doctrinal matters, the friendship between him and his younger colleague took precedence in their later years together. It wasn't until after Charles V finally defeated the Schmalkald League, in the later 1540s, that Melanchthon's theological revisions resulted in open theological conflict among Lutheran theologians. Then it was almost thirty years, in 1577, before the issues were settled, in the *Formula of Concord.*

RECONCILIATIONS ON THE UPPER RHINE

Though the Lutherans had agreed to go it alone at the Diet of Augsburg, they were still vulnerable—even after the formation of the Schmalkald League. Charles V was still a formidable threat. If the Nuremburg Standstill offered a respite, it was clearly temporary, providing an opportunity to build a larger alliance, this time one that would include the Upper Rhine or southwest Germans and the Swiss. If the goal was primarily political, formulating an agreement would be largely theological.

Maybe the politicians would have been better off keeping matters in their own hands. From the beginning, Luther's religious protest had struck a political chord—political and religious concerns had combined with social and economic factors to propel the Reformation. When Luther appealed to the German nobility to help in the reform, they stepped forward eagerly. So, following the Diet of Augsburg, they redoubled their efforts, promoting the Wittenberg reforms in their own territories as they expanded the Schmalkald League. In the process, they learned to step around some of the differences among the theologians, gaining just enough agreement to work together.

Still, as the Lutheran reform expanded, its adherents generally followed the pattern in Wittenberg. Disgusted with the religious excesses of the medieval church, which had sought to control virtually every aspect of life, the politicians wanted to exercise the same kind of liberty that the electors had. Taking a direct hand in the life of the church, they organized visitations and, while leaving religious matters in the hands of the pastors, made arrangements for the practicalities. The eventual result was state-church Lutheranism, a system in which virtually all citizens are considered church members. The state maintains the church economically, while pastors and other church leaders have a relatively free hand. This set-up has prevailed until recently in the parts of Germany that remained Lutheran and in Scandinavia, although changes are now underway.

Luther was directly involved in spreading the Reformation, though as usual it was sporadic. Sometimes it was through his friends, like Bugenhagen, who carried the reform to Denmark and through the Danes to Norway and Iceland. Sometimes it was through students like Michael Agricola, who, after his time in Wittenberg, went back to Turku, in Western Finland, and translated both the Bible and the *Small Catechism* into Finnish. Sometimes, it was by consultation, either in person with politicians who took up temporary residence in the Black Cloister or through correspondence. It was by consultation that after some stops and starts Sweden, through its royalty, aligned itself with the Lutheran reform. Luther had become a reformer by accident; he had no interest in starting a separate church and no model constitutions or plans for ideal structures. But in the meantime, he would make do with the possibilities that presented themselves to spread the Gospel.

As the Lutheran reform and the Schmalkald League expanded, the most significant obstacle, aside from the traditional Roman Catholic authorities, was still the southwest Germans and the Swiss. The difference of opinion between Luther and Ulrich Zwingli still blocked the way, even though early in the 1530s Zwingli was killed in a Swiss war. His place was taken by Heinrich Bullinger. The farther south and west in Germany the Lutheran reform went, the more resistance it found.

The issue was still the Eucharist. Martin Bucer of Strasbourg, a former Augustinian whom Luther had first met in Heidelberg in 1518, took a leading role in the new negotiations with the southwest Germans and the Swiss. Sometimes Luther was harsh, describing his opponents as heretics. Sometimes he was conciliatory, accepting softer language from the Bohemian Brethren and the church in Augsburg in 1535 that described Christ's presence in the sacrament. He wasn't always confident of Bucer, either. Once, Bucer having walked all the way to Wittenberg, Luther let him wait for a couple of weeks, refusing even to see him. But through the early 1530s Bucer went back and forth among the parties, putting Luther's arguments in the kindest light to the Upper Rhine Germans and Swiss while at the same time trying to placate Luther's concerns. Bucer's best support in Wittenberg came from Melanchthon, who had his heart set on the reconciliation.

Along the way, the issues shifted, growing more complex. The basic disagreement was always the nature of Christ's presence in the sacrament. Luther insisted on the down-to-earth identity of Christ's body and blood with the bread and the wine, while the others spoke of it more symbolically. They were willing to say that the bread and wine "exhibit" or "display" Christ's true body and blood. But, as Luther saw it, that still left an opening for ambiguity. As the issue developed, the "eating of the impious" also was contested. Luther argued that because the crucified and risen Christ is actually present in the elements (the bread and wine) the faithful and even the unfaithful—the impious—meet him there. Luther's opponents insisted that, because faith is necessary to interpret the symbol, the impious get nothing more than bread and wine. Finally, the focus shifted to Christ's divine and human natures. Luther argued that the divine shares itself with the human as the human shares itself with the divine, so that Christ is eucharistically present in his humanity. The Upper Rhine and Swiss theologians argued that the human limits the divine, so that in his humanity, Christ cannot be everywhere present.

With Bucer shuttling back and forth virtually full-time, braving the opposition on both sides, what appeared to be a final resolution occurred in 1536. Called the Wittenberg Concord, it had all the characteristics of ecumenical agreements—basically, an agreement to disagree. With Melanchthon's firm support, Luther accepted it. It looked as though the conversations begun years earlier at Marburg had finally borne fruit.

But this time, the Swiss were reluctant. Offended by what they took to be Luther's high-handedness on the matter, they compared Luther with the pope. Although Bucer continued his efforts for several years, the Swiss opposition forestalled acceptance of the Wittenberg Concord. It died on the vine. It wasn't until late in the twentieth century that the heirs of Luther and the Reformed were able to formulate agreement on the Lord's Supper.

TOWARD A COUNCIL: TROUBLES ON THE CATHOLIC SIDE

In 1534 Pope Clement went to his eternal reward and was replaced by Paul III. Clement had done everything possible to protect papal prerogatives, blocking any positive change or reformation in any form. Though his successor, Paul III, was not any more positively disposed to the Reformers, he at least recognized that changes had to be made. Slowly, with the glacial pace characteristic of large-scale institutions, Roman Catholicism began to turn from mere reaction. Even if the turn was still not positive for the Lutherans, the church was finally beginning to stir itself.

Having committed himself to supporting a church council and having negotiated the Nuremburg Standstill, Charles V leveraged what advantage he could to get Paul III to summon a council. In 1536, he succeeded. To be sure, the pope made it crystal clear that he wasn't envisioning anything free or open. In announcing the council, he declared its purpose as "the utter extirpation of the poisonous and pestilential Lutheran heresy." But even so, after almost two decades of appeal and effort, a council was actually going to meet.

The scheduled council occasioned some debate in Wittenberg. Given the pope's expressed purpose, those who opposed attending such a council had good reasons to do so. Even the proposed location, at Mantua, in Italy, was clearly set so that the pope could maintain close control. On the other hand, having agreed to accept Charles's efforts, and concerned that the Reformation not end in a breach of church unity, those who supported attending the council argued for cooperation. While the debate went back and forth, there was enough possibility of attendance to warrant preparations. So Luther was instructed to draw up a statement that could be presented to the council.

The question of such a statement was itself divisive. The *Augsburg Confession* had nearly resulted in settlement and won widespread recognition. The two Philips, Melanchthon and Philip of Hesse, favored using it again. Others, including Luther himself, wanted something more direct and plain-spoken. Sovereigns who had aligned themselves with the Schmalkald League since 1530 also wanted a chance to participate more directly. Luther, convinced that he was in his last days, wanted a chance to make one more confession. The result was an instruction from the Elector of Saxony to Luther to write the document.

Luther started at the beginning of December 1536. He had been feeling good, he was in full command of his gifts, and he was delighted with the prospect. Working steadily, in just over two weeks he finished the bulk of what has come to be called the *Schmalkald Articles*. At that point, December 18, he suffered another heart attack. Though it turned out to be minor, he was bedridden for the rest of the month, possibly into January of 1537. Melanchthon and the other Wittenberg Reformers visited him during this time. He managed to complete the document by dictation, and his statement was approved. The tone was polemical, expansive, and always transparently direct. It was almost immediately recognized as another one of Luther's classic confessions.

The quality of Luther's work didn't resolve the question of attendance at the council, however. In February of 1537, the politicians of the Schmalkald League assembled to consider the issue. In the process, the realities of the situation undermined more abstract concerns for the unity of the church. No matter what agreement had been made with Charles, it appeared that the council was clearly not going to be free or open or even universal. The Italian bishops, under the pope's lead, would control everything. So League leaders decided not to attend. In the end, after some parliamentary maneuvering by Melanchthon and Philip of Hesse, the *Schmalkald Articles* were not even formally considered. They were circulated informally. Melanchthon indicated that he was willing to accept the papacy, providing it was recognized as a merely human office—a manifestly impossible condition.

Convinced that Luther had to be there for the League meeting, no matter what his condition, Elector John Frederick had made arrangements to transport him to Torgau. In the meantime, perhaps before he reached there, perhaps during the assembly, Luther suffered a terrible attack of kidney stones—one of the worst ever. In the end, the elector sent him back to Wittenberg, jostling and screaming in agony along the mountain roads in a specially constructed but still rough-riding cart. That jolting ride apparently saved him. Luther joked afterward about the "precious liquid" that he passed.

Due, among other things, to the Schmalkald League's refusal to attend, the council was postponed. After many delays, a council finally was summoned by a new pope, beginning in the city of Trent and carrying on, in fits and starts, from 1545 until 1563. The Italian bishops had the votes from the very beginning, with some Spanish and French representation. There was no Lutheran representation. In the early sessions, the Reformers' arguments were dismissed out of hand, under the rationale that it was not necessary to examine the views of heretics.

Though it did little to improve relations with Lutheran Christians, the Council of Trent, especially in later sessions, was an important force in the reformation of Catholicism itself. With its changes, Roman Catholicism took on another identity, known as Tridentine from the city of its origin.

Today the familial similarities between Lutheranism and its Roman Catholic origins show through the differences. Taken by such continuities, many contemporary Lutherans stress what is common, minimizing the differences. Clearly, if Luther had had his own way, a council would have met to overcome the division, holding the church together as one. But Luther's intentions and hopes cannot be separated from the many forces, positive or negative, originating in Rome or Wittenberg, that resulted in the formation of Lutheranism as a separate church.

POLITICS: THE BEGINNING OF THE END

While the theologians were sounding out their disagreements, the politicians were making some important changes.

Through the 1520s, Luther had been able to rely on the Saxon electors—even if he didn't know them personally—first, Frederick the Wise, and after 1525, his brother John the Constant. In 1532, John's son, John Frederick, took over. In Luther's mind, the young elector was a mixed blessing. On the one hand, Luther knew him better than he had John Frederick's predecessors. John Frederick had been a student in Wittenberg and was a convinced Lutheran. John Frederick stayed in contact with Luther, by letter generally, though Luther sometimes went to visit him at the court in Torgau. As he matured, John Frederick proved himself an effective leader. On the other hand, the elector had a problem familiar to politicians and around many homes: he liked alcohol—a lot. Luther never made any secret of his own enjoyment of alcohol, but he disapproved of drunkenness strongly and regularly chided John Frederick for his abuses. Still, they stayed on good terms.

From early on, Duke George—the elector's counterpart in the other part of Saxony—had been one of Luther's most ardent enemies, but in 1539 Duke George died. His successor, Maurice of Saxony, had both personal and political reasons for aligning his territory with the Reformation. When he did, it solidified the Schmalkald League's standing in east and south-central Germany, giving them a more united front. Later on, his political aspiration overrode his religious convictions—at least for a time—and in attempting to reunite the two parts of Saxony, he dealt the Schmalkald League a serious blow. But for the time being, it looked as if he were adding strength to strength.

If they didn't watch Maurice as closely as they might have, John Frederick and Philip of Hesse knew enough to keep an eye on the emperor. This was especially necessary after they refused to attend the council scheduled for Mantua, thereby breaching terms of the Nuremburg Standstill. Though the League was strong, Charles V was a worthy opponent with enough power to make good his military threat.

For this reason, the Wittenberg theologians went back to the question of resistance. In the 1520s, Luther had been convinced that fighting fire with fire just spread the flame—as in the Peasants' War. In the early 1530s, he had conceded, however reluctantly, that in certain limited instances armed resistance might be necessary. Melanchthon was still hesitant, arguing the necessity of obedience to the emperor. But in the later 1530s, Luther saw an impending and catastrophic combination of papal and imperial power. For several years, he had been sympathetic to an old medieval tradition that linked the papacy with the Antichrist, and he described the papacy in just such terms. Seeking to maintain power, the pope was undermining the Gospel, Luther believed; and the emperor was linking arms with the pontiff. In such a circumstance, the faithful must follow the biblical Book of Acts, obeying God rather than human institutions. If it came to force, force would have to do.

So as the 1530s came to an end, Luther's end-time expectations flared. He was reading the Book of Daniel and other biblical imagery of the end of the world. They matched his own sense of things, of being embattled on all sides and of imminent doom. Melanchthon was turning the reform in more humanistic directions. Luther's old friend Agricola had turned on him and left town. The Swiss were blocking agreement on the sacrament. He had given up on councils, convinced that they, too, were error-prone. And while fighting his own health problems, he was getting a bellyful of moral breakdown, both in the Wittenberg congregation and the Saxon court. And there, once more, was the emperor, poised to make good on this threats. If Christ didn't come soon, there would be no telling how things would end.

CHAPTER 10

THE END AND THE BEGINNING

According to legend, Luther was asked what he would do if he knew that the world were going to end tomorrow. "Plant an apple tree," he is alleged to have said. According to another account, he replied that he would take his wife, Katherine, to bed. Either way, he wanted God to find him doing what human beings do. Luther was down to earth.

In fact, by just about any account, Luther's behavior in the 1540s was altogether too human. He continued his work with Scripture, teaching, writing, revising his translation. It is still possible to see some of the spirit that had driven him through the earlier years. But he was also old, tired, frequently ill, and increasingly impatient. His writing more often showed bitterness and invective. If that puts in perspective some of his hostile and malicious writings against the Jews and the Catholics, it certainly doesn't justify or excuse them. Luther's angel and his demon had long contended within him; now, more than occasionally, the angel lost, and the Reformer's power with language became horribly destructive, particularly by our standards. When Martin Luther died in 1546, the Reformation legacy was in deep jeopardy.

SICK AND TIRED OF BEING SICK AND TIRED

Luther was still at his best in the classroom. Along with the Psalms and the letters of Paul, the Gospel of John, and 1 Peter, the Book of Genesis drew Luther deeply. So in 1535 he started a series of lectures on the book, commenting on it chapter by chapter, verse by verse. He continued for nine years, completing the fiftieth chapter in 1545.

Unfortunately, the published text of Luther's lectures isn't completely reliable. Luther was opposed to printing the lectures—he thought they were meandering and discursive. Initially, some of his best editors got hold of the notes and put them together. But then in the 1550s, some of Melanchthon's students, eager to stress the continuity between Luther and Melanchthon's efforts at reinterpretation, added their own hands to the text. As a result, the commentary does not faithfully represent his work.

Still, Luther's Genesis commentary does convey the full flavor of Luther's engagement with the book. The original narrative is rich and full of life, moving from creation and fall, to the flood and the tower of Babel, then on to Abraham and Sarah, Isaac and Rebekah, Esau, Jacob and his family, and finally to Joseph and his brothers. Luther moved slowly, amplifying the account with experiential and biblical parallels. He identified particularly with Jacob, finding in the narrative of the patriarch's blessings and reversals similarities to his own struggles. Even toward the end of the commentary, when Luther was nearing the end of his own life, he was capable of seeing the deeper religious truth in the biblical narrative. An example is his comment on the doctrine of repentance, which spelled out the hardness of Joseph's brothers in their recourse to deceit and Joseph's graciousness in blessing them.

While lecturing on Genesis, Luther finished his last revisions of his Bible translation. It had gotten to be a group process, with Melanchthon and several others on the faculty at Wittenberg contributing. His last translation was completed in the mid-1530s, but Luther, alone or sometimes with his colleagues, kept going back to touch things up. The last revisions appeared in 1544.

The classroom and his study must have been some respite for the old man. Other duties still delivered daily doses of contention. He was still consulted about, though he didn't often directly participate in, the spread of the reform—dealing with the frustrations and roadblocks. He also had a hand in the care of the Saxon Church, complaining regularly—among other things—about the poor salaries paid to the preachers. When his health allowed, he took a regular turn in the pulpit of the city church. It was a reduced load: in one of his last years, he preached some thirty-five times, which was minimal compared to years past. Even with his age and burdens, he was still capable of a good sermon.

Dealings with the Wittenberg congregation had a way of becoming especially nettlesome in the 1540s. Luther was not a moralist. Earlier on, when he had received reports of some of his students taking town prostitutes out to the woods, he reportedly called them in and instead of scolding them, asked if he wasn't giving them enough work.

to do that they had time for such pursuits. But in his later years, he found common immoral behavior uncommonly trying. Sometimes it was public drunkenness, including the elector's; sometimes common sexual adventuring of students and townspeople triggered his ire. More often the precipitating issue was greed. Still compulsively generous despite his health and his family's financial struggles, he was particularly sensitive to violations of the commandment against stealing. Shoddy merchandise, inflated prices, high interest rates (which in his mind started around 3 percent), and miserliness were common breaches that Luther inveighed against regularly.

In 1545, Luther's impatience with moral lapses peaked. Earlier, he had grown so disgusted with the Wittenberg congregation that he effectively went on strike, refusing to preach. That summer, away on a trip, he wrote to Katherine von Bora that he wasn't going to return, citing people's immorality, among other things the low bodices the women were wearing, as a reason to stay away. Officials prevailed upon him to come home, but he returned full of the impatience that had driven his alienation.

Clearly, Luther's health didn't help his temperament. For a time in the early 1540s and again in 1545, he felt relatively good. But his kidney troubles, by this time causing physical distortions that can be seen in a plaster cast of his hands taken at the time of his death, still came and went. Headaches sometimes incapacitated him. The ringing in his ears, dizziness, fainting spells, and fatigue were common maladies. He often felt as if death were just around the corner. Sometimes he longed to be done with it all. He relied heavily on Katherine von Bora through it all, generally trusting her judgment in such matters, but he wasn't as confident of the doctors. At one point, he remarked that what they really needed with all their treatments was a new cemetery.

Several times, most dramatically in February 1537, Luther was completely blocked by kidney stones, suffering uremic poisoning as a result. Uremia at that level has been known medically to make people irritable and short-tempered, prone to outbursts. Again, that fact cannot be used to justify or explain away Luther's behavior or judgments, but it does put his temperamental outbursts into perspective.

SOME VICIOUS ATTACKS

While Luther's Wittenberg congregation, his family, and colleagues witnessed his growing impatience firsthand, more distant opponents suffered his barbs in print. Two essays in particular show him close to his worst, one against a political figure and the other a last attack on the papacy.

The politician was Henry of Brunswick-Wolfenbüttel, an old friend of Charles V, who had been a harsh opponent of the Reformation. Late in the 1530s, he had exchanged hostilities with John Frederick and Philip of Hesse in their capacities as leaders of the Schmalkald League. Defending his actions, he wrote a nasty piece against Luther in which he claimed that Luther had referred to John Frederick as his "Hanswurst"—a grotesque, carnival clown popular in Germany. With this, Luther felt duty-bound to reply, matching invectives one for one. When in 1541 Luther responded to Henry's attack, describing him as the real Hans Wurst, he became as crude as he was tender in other connections. "My dear Hans," he wrote, "you should have listened to a fart from an old sow and opened your mouth wide to it and said, 'Thank you, sweet nightingale, that will make a good text for me.'"

If the exchange with Henry was finally inconsequential, Luther's outburst against the pope was considerably more offensive. Just the title, *Against the Papacy: An Institution of the Devil,* was enough to send shock waves. Luther had held on to the hope of ecumenical reconciliation long into the 1530s, even when he knew full well that the possibilities were slim. When he had heard that what became the Council of Trent was beginning to meet, he considered sending a portrait of himself and Katherine von Bora. But in 1545, in this last bitter essay, all of his disappointments, including further delay of the council's convening, were focused. Charged with the promulgation of the Gospel, the papacy had completely reversed its purpose, becoming demonic in the process. Luther had Lucas Cranach, the Wittenberg painter and woodcut artist, illustrate the text. In one graphic, as the cardinals look on, the pope is preparing to be hanged. Whatever else might be said about this essay, Luther had clearly had it with the papacy.

LUTHER AND THE JEWS

Although they didn't draw nearly as much attention as his other polemics at the time, in more recent years Luther's early 1540s writings on the Jews have become the most notorious. The Nazis and other anti-Semites have used them for their own purposes. The Holocaust Museum in Washington, D.C., has prominently displayed a quotation from *Against the Jews and Their Lies*—the first and best known of three essays. Luther is commonly considered an anti-Semite. As unacceptable as some of his statements are, however, examined closely, the issue of Luther's attitude toward the Jews is considerably more complex.

In late medieval Europe, as now in many other parts of the world, life was inherently communal. Every attempt was made to protect the cohesiveness of the community from individual differences. Muslims and Jews were the only minorities considered capable of undermining that necessary unity. Islam threatened Europe from its southern corners—Turkish Muslims in the southeast and the Arabian Muslims in the west—before being forced back in the High Middle Ages. The Jews, originally more widely dispersed in medieval Europe, were like the ethnic Chinese in Southeast Asia or ethnic Indians in Africa, who are frequently involved in business enterprises and money lending, on the margins of society. In such connections, the Jews were considered a more internal threat. The Crusades of the Middle Ages were mounted to protect the unity of Europe as Christendom. On their way to the Middle East to reclaim the Holy Lands from Islam, the Crusaders practiced their skills by murdering Jews in Europe.

The church gave full support. A thirteenth-century council required all Jews to identify themselves publicly by wearing marks on their clothing. More commonly, the favored strategy was expulsion. Spain, France, and England all expelled the Jews; early in the fifteenth century, Austria and several German communities followed suit. In 1536, though the immediate reasons for his action aren't known, John Frederick expelled the Jews from electoral Saxony.

In 1523, Luther had written a treatise entitled *That Jesus Christ Was Born a Jew,* which was widely regarded as friendly to Judaism. In it, Luther expressed the conviction that Jews persisted in their faith because they hadn't yet had an opportunity to hear God's word, the Gospel, fully. In the context, Jews took it as an enlightened statement, and it was apparently translated and circulated as far away as Spain and possibly even Palestine. It didn't necessarily win Luther any friends among traditional Roman Catholics, however. Among others, Johann Eck considered Luther soft on Judaism.

In the mid-1530s, Luther met with three rabbis who came to Wittenberg to talk with him about his interpretation of passages in the Old Testament. Christians have traditionally read such passages in the light of Jesus Christ; the rabbis read them otherwise, in the light of their own tradition. The discussions didn't go very far. In 1536, Luther was contacted by Josel of Rosheim, the officially designated spokesman of

Judaism in the empire. He asked for help with a safe conduct, given John Frederick's expulsion. Luther refused.

In May 1542, the issue of Judaism arose once more, this time in a letter from a friend asking his response to an essay written by a Jew in conversation with a Christian. The essay challenged Christian interpretation of the Old Testament and the claim that Jesus is the Messiah. Though there may have been other factors not completely known, this was the occasion for Luther's three 1543 essays—first *On the Jews and Their Lies,* then *On the Ineffable Name and on Christ's Lineage,* and finally, *On the Last Words of David.* Most of the three writings are dedicated to theological arguments, either refuting what Luther considered to be Jewish attacks or establishing Christian claims concerning the Virgin Mary, Jesus the Messiah, and the Trinity. But in the first essay, Luther digressed to endorse the harsh measures taken by several European rulers and communities against the Jews, including expulsion and the burning of synagogues. In the second, Luther gets vulgar at points, dismissing Jewish claims as excrement. In the third, he is more careful to stick to the theological points he is making.

Was Luther an anti-Semite? Clearly, by common contemporary standards, his harsh judgments, along with the vulgarities, are seriously objectionable, if not downright indefensible. Contemporary American Lutherans, in fact, have issued a public apology for his statements. But that acknowledged, there are some common elements of historical anti-Semitism missing from Luther's writings. For all of the theological arguments and invective, there are no racial references. In Luther's mind a converted Jew was a brother or sister in Christ, differences of ethnic background notwithstanding. The standard charges of medieval anti-Judaism—accusation of well poisonings, forced circumcisions, kidnappings of Christian children for sacrifices, and the like, are also missing. Like his predecessors and contemporaries, including Martin Bucer, Luther clearly did not regard Judaism as a legitimate religious alternative, one valid religion among many. Even if sometimes restrained, his invective other times was excessive and harmful in his theological critiques. Today it is clear that Luther's statements, even if theologically rather than racially motivated, have been one element in the centuries-long negative portrayal of the Jews that influenced their fate in Europe, right up to the Holocaust.

Finally, as noticeable a part as Luther's temperament played in the controversies of the 1540s, for him there were clearly other considerations justifying unusual measures. Whether it was Henry or Hanswurst, the papacy or the Jews, there were genuine theological issues at stake—matters pertaining to proper thinking about the Gospel. And the times had become increasingly apocalyptic, not only in Luther's mind but in those around him. Luther's invective reflects his premonitions of disaster.

CALAMITY IN THE LEAGUE

Entering the 1540s, the Schmalkald League was in a strong position, the alliance expanding, its enemies contracting under the leadership of Philip of Hesse. But in 1539, Philip's bedroom made the news in reports that eventually compromised his leadership. Bucer and Melanchthon were implicated in the mess, Luther with them. And more serious problems developed that would make the League vulnerable to attack from Charles V.

Married to the daughter of Duke George, who coincidentally died in 1539, Philip generally didn't miss the other romantic or sexual opportunities available to him. That year he wanted to marry a beautiful seventeen-year-old. But, unlike his English counterpart, Henry VIII, Philip didn't ask for divorce. He proposed something different: that, like the patriarchs of the Old Testament, he should practice polygamy. Philip approached Martin Bucer, who in turn contacted Philip Melanchthon. They consulted Luther.

Everybody involved in the situation knew what was right, including Philip himself. But life gets more complicated than the law, and so pastors, particularly in the confessional, sometimes make adjustments. Luther, a wise old pastor even if a sick one, had learned to be realistic. So he, along with his partners in the matter, accepted Philip of Hesse's proposal, with the consent of Philip's wife. As they saw it, better a bigamist than a philanderer, but they insisted that the second marriage be entered in secret.

Philip accepted the theologians' terms, even if he didn't go to any great length to preserve the secrecy. The wedding was at least semi-public, and soon, as might be expected, word began to get out. When it finally reached Charles V, Philip of Hesse was in a real jam. Even though widely and openly flaunted, bigamy was illegal, and there were moral standards to be expected of the politicians of the empire—and the emperor was responsible for their enforcement. Slyly, Charles agreed not to prosecute Philip; in exchange Philip agreed to take no more role in opposing the emperor's plans for religious reunion of the empire. The League was severely damaged.

The scandal nearly cost Melanchthon his life. When word of his implication in the situation got out, he was overwhelmed and took to his bed, depressed almost to death. When Luther heard of it, he paid his younger colleague a pastoral visit. As he had done earlier when Philip and Barbara had lost a child, he threw open the window and in an old phrase, got a hold of God by the whiskers. Reminding the good Lord of the promises in Scripture to hear prayer, Luther insisted on Melanchthon's recovery. Shortly thereafter, Melanchthon was back on his feet.

A further serious weakening of the Schmalkald League developed in a more effectively kept secret, at least until it was too late. Though he had been forced to withhold his hand through the 1530s and into the 1540s, Charles V had still not given up on restoring the religious unity of the empire. Looking for chinks in the League's armor, he had been gathering a fellowship of discontent—members who for one reason or another might be willing to compromise their support. He found one in Maurice of Saxony (successor to Duke George), who regretted the division of the two Saxonys and as duke also wanted to take over as elector. Despite his own religious convictions, Maurice made a deal with Charles, giving him military support in exchange for that outcome. Maurice's treachery dealt a body blow to the Schmalkald League.

LUTHER'S DEATH

Meanwhile, family loyalties—and taxes—drew Luther back to Eisleben, the city of his birth, in the winter of 1546. When Luther had joined the monastery, his brother had stayed behind to tend the family business in copper. The Count of Mansfeld, seeking greater income, had levied a greater tax. Over Katherine von Bora's objections, Luther went to help mediate the conflict. At her insistence, two of their boys went along. So did Justus Jonas.

Writing to his beloved wife, Luther teased her about her anxieties. The boys were bored and went visiting, perhaps with their cousins. And the negotiations, predictably, took longer than expected. Luther and his company remained at an inn in the city.

Things went fairly well until the evening of February 17, when Luther suffered a heart attack about 8:00 in the evening. He was at prayer. Receiving some medication, he slept briefly and then at 10:00 went to bed. At that time, he prayed Psalm 31:5, a verse commonly used by the dying, "Into your hands I commit my spirit; you have redeemed me, O Lord, faithful God." He also joked with his friends that they had better pray for the good Lord, given the trouble he was having with the pope and the Council of Trent.

Awakening again at 1:00 A.M. with sharp pain, Luther was attended by Dr. Jonas, a pastor from Mansfeld, and some officials, including the count and his wife. Luther did not ask for the last rites. He repeated Psalm 31:5 three times, at which point he fell silent.

There were various attempts to revive Luther. At one point either Jonas or the pastor, possibly both of them together, called to him, asking if he was still willing to confess the faith he had taught in Christ's name. Luther answered with a clear yes and said no more. At about 2:45 A.M. on February 18, Luther passed away.

Three funerals were held, two on successive days in Eisleben and a third in Wittenberg. Jonas preached at first in Eisleben, mentioning in particular Luther's work in translating the Bible. Michael Coelius, the Mansfeld pastor who had been present at Luther's death, preached at the second. John Frederick insisted, over the count's objections, that the body be returned to Wittenberg to be buried not in the city church but in the castle church. Villages along the way tolled the church bells as the procession moved through on the way back to Wittenberg.

At the Wittenberg funeral, John Bugenhagen preached and Philip Melanchthon delivered the eulogy. Both of them numbered Luther with the prophets and the patriarchs. Bugenhagen, struggling to maintain his composure, also used the term *reformer* to speak of Luther's efforts to restore the Gospel to its proper priority. Melanchthon, in announcing Luther's death to the students, had used Elisha's words concerning Elijah: "Gone is the charioteer of Israel." Now he acknowledged frankly some of his difficulties with Luther, particularly his "harsh manner of speech" and his teaching on the bound will, but he also spoke of Luther's immense contribution in recovering the church's doctrine, describing him as having gone to the great university in heaven, where he was now seeing the fulfillment of his hopes.

In the centuries following Luther's death, not everyone has agreed with the appraisals of Luther's friends. Still a hugely controversial figure, Luther has generated libraries of scholarship, both for and against. In popular culture, both in Northern Europe and in North America, he has retained the symbolic power that he gained at and after the Diet of Worms in 1521. Sometimes the symbol is negative, Luther being regarded as the archetype of broken church unity, intolerance, and doctrinaire prejudice. But more often he is regarded as a symbol of freedom, the awakening of a critical spirit willing to test established powers in light of deep conviction and a divine word.

THE END OF THE REFORMATION

After Luther's death, Charles V brought his Spanish troops across the Alps and in 1547 went to war against the Schmalkald League. The emperor made short work of it. Though the League had superior forces, Charles managed to split their armies into manageable pieces. There was only one real battle, at Mulburg in April 1547. Charles won it decisively, his Spanish troops marching across Katherine von Bora's farms, destroying everything, moving right into Wittenberg. Both John Frederick and Philip of Hesse were captured. The two Saxonys were reunited. For all intents and purposes, it seemed the Lutheran Reformation had finally come to an end.

Yet like an aging boxer, Charles had the power to put his opponent on the ropes but not to knock him out. Defeating the Schmalkald League, he was forced to temporize, first making minimal concessions that had originally been discussed at Augsburg in 1530 and then having to withdraw. Having changed colors once, Maurice of Saxony, known as "the Judas of the Reformation," made a habit of it. Charles's fellowship of discontent fell apart. When the opportunity arose, Maurice's original convictions reasserted themselves, and he chased Charles right out of Germany. A preliminary peace was made in Passau in 1552; final terms were agreed to at the Peace of Augsburg in 1555. Lutheranism became a legally recognized state church.

Even from the grave, Luther played a significant part in Charles V's final failure. Translating the Bible into German, translating his theology into the language and thought of the people, Luther had in significant portions of Germany and in Scandinavia ignited rebellion and reform. In the end, even if Charles could defeat the League, he couldn't reverse decades of reform. The Lutheran Reformation had become firmly established in the hearts of the people.

After his death, Luther's colleague theologians fought a desperate series of conflicts over his legacy on a host of theological issues. Melanchthon's theological revisions were a significant factor in what he at one point termed "the rabies of the theologians." His more loyal students remained with him in Wittenberg until his death in 1561—and were called the Philippists. His opponents, led by Nicolas von Amsdorf and one of the great curmudgeons of later Lutheranism, a Croatian named Matthias Flacius Illyricus, withdrew first of all to the city of Magdeburg and then, forced out of there, wandered. Called the "Gnesio-Lutherans," from their claim to be Luther's real heirs, they attacked Melanchthon vituperously.

The conflicts were finally settled in the *Formula of Concord* of 1577, which sought to restore Luther's theological conclusions on the basis of Melanchthon's theological methods. As a result, the tradition was both preserved and reshaped, as it has been again and again since. Despite all of the powers ranged against him, Luther's legacy survived not only his detractors but also his followers in a tradition that is always reforming.

What, in the end, are we to make of Martin Luther? What people think of themselves is not always an accurate measure. But Luther was remarkably frank about himself. His last written words were: "We are beggars. This is the truth." He was a sinner, just as he said. Many things that he said and did establish no precedent, especially in a changed and changing world. At the same time, he understood himself to be what he was called to be by the God who raised Jesus from the dead, through the agencies of the church: a pastor, a doctor of theology called to serve the proclamation of the Gospel. For that purpose, he spent every effort. And at just this point, he continues to be useful to us. Even though he was a great emancipator, whose words and deeds have had momentous consequences around the world, they stemmed from his personal struggles to understand himself religiously. Luther's deep insights into the problems and potential of human freedom still echo today, clearly conveying the place of the law and God's promise in Christ to forgive sins, to raise the dead, and to bind the powers of desolation.

Other Resources on Martin Luther

Martin Luther: Exploring His Life and Times, 1483-15
CD-ROM by Helmar Junghans
0-8006-3147-1

This CD-ROM brings alive the universe of Martin
Luther in his own place and time, from birth to dea
between heaven and hell through graphics and narr.

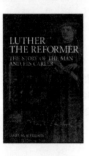

Luther the Reformer: The Story of the Man and His Career
by James Kittelson
334 pages, 0-8006-3597-3

Kittleson's single-volume biography has become a stand.
resource for those who wish to delve into the depths of t
Reformer without drowning in a sea of scholarly concer.

My Conversations with Martin Luther by Timothy F. Lul
96 pages, 0-8066-3898-2

Lull offers Luther's pithy observations on such timely
topics as the family and sexuality, roles of men and
women, enemies and friends, renewal in the church, politics and ecumenism, interpretation of the Bible, and the
resistance of congregations to the Gospel message.

Three Treatises by Martin Luther
316 pages, 0-8006-1639-1

Martin Luther posted his Ninety-five Theses on the chu
door at Wittenberg in 1517. In the three years that follo
Luther clarified and defended his position in numerous
ings. Chief among these are the three treatises written i
1520. In these writings Luther tried to frame his ideas i
terms that would be comprehensible not only to the cle
but to people from a wide range of backgrounds.

Available wherever books are sold.